WITH GRACE
AND GRATITUDE

WITH GRACE AND GRATITUDE

A Memoir of Uncoupling, Co-Parenting, and Collective Healing

Meg Campbell

Book Cover by Shera Lynn Studio

ISBN: 979-8-89316-240-0 (Paperback)
ISBN: 979-8-89316-239-4 (Hardcover)
ISBN: 979-8-89316-241-7 (Ebook)

Meg Campbell Coaching, LLC

www.megcampbellcoaching.com

For everyone who values loving big, living gently and letting go gracefully. May reading these words facilitate some of the healing I found in writing them.

CONTENTS

PART 4: 2019

PART 5: 2020

PART 1

THE MIDDLE

Wrecked and Rescued

> One ends a romantic relationship while remaining a compassionate friend by being kind above all else. By explaining one's decision to leave the relationship with love and respect and emotional transparency. By being honest without being brutal. By expressing gratitude for what was given. By taking responsibility for mistakes and attempting to make amends. By acknowledging that one's decision has caused another human being to suffer. By suffering because of that. By having the guts to stand by one's partner even while one is leaving. By talking it all the way through and by listening. By honoring what once was. By bearing witness to the undoing and salvaging what one can. By being a friend, even if an actual friendship is impossible. By having good manners. By considering how one might feel if the tables were turned. By going out of one's way to minimize hurt and humiliation. By trusting that the most compassionate thing of all is to release those we don't love hard enough or true enough or big enough or right. By believing we are all worthy of hard, true, big, right love. By remembering while letting go. (Strayed 2015, 130-31)

Every so often I come across something that completely and simultaneously wrecks and rescues me. I've been a big Cheryl Strayed fan for a long time, but coming across this advice years ago absolutely stopped me cold. I needed a minute, that turned into years, to absorb the most painfully true thing I'd ever read. I'd go on to read this quote over and over and over again in the months and years that followed. It spoke to my core, but living in the state of scarcity I was so accustomed to at the time and still defaulting to my fear-based decision-making model, I didn't know what to do with this kind of wisdom. I couldn't even wrap my head around the idea that such an ending to a romantic relationship, my marriage specifically, might be possible. A decade later I am incredibly grateful, beyond fortunate, and pretty dang proud to know better.

The Middle

Beginning, middle, end. I've taught my fair share of story element lessons. This book is a glimpse into the middle of my divorce story. I'm not ready to write the beginning. While I get into past and personal history relevant to my divorce recovery—as far as the how, the why, the various factors and intricate pieces that ultimately ended a marriage—those aren't addressed here. I'm tempted to say maybe someday. Or maybe it'll feel unnecessary or unimportant later. Right now, my rumbling with and unpacking the content of some earlier chapters is ongoing and painful, not ready to be shaped into words.

As for the ending, I like to think of this passion project as a step in the right direction toward my own daring ending. Hat tip to Brené Brown (2012): researcher, educator, storyteller, big influencer of my own journey, reminding us that we're the authors of our lives. I know better now than to guess in much detail what the future holds, and I still have plenty of work to do when it comes to not ruminating over the past or worrying about what's next and simply existing in the now. All I feel certain of anymore is the huge love I feel for my three kids and for this one spectacular life. What a gift—this relatively short window in which I get to experience loving, losing, hurting, healing, living, and trying to navigate it all with more grace and gratitude.

This is an account of living through divorce. More than simply surviving the experience, but about doing it differently, vulnerably, and shaping our "happily *even* after" (Thomas 2016). It's not all that novel of a story, which used to make me think I'd never share it outside of my own mind or Google Drive. We humans love to explore healing, transformative pain, and growth out of despair—perhaps searching for a quicker fix or obvious answer to something as prevalent as heartache, perhaps simply hoping to better understand such universal experiences.

We share, read, listen to, and cherish these stories. I have needed and leaned on them plenty—stories of resilience when I'm broken, of perseverance when I'm ready to give up, reminders that love and connection exist and are worth moving toward when I'm feeling impossibly lost and alone. That recollection of a story I once heard or read of someone surviving the seemingly unsurvivable is powerful. Just as others' words and stories have wrecked and rescued me, I'm putting this out there, absolutely terrified but also hopeful and humble at the thought it might support another.

I know my experience of divorce well and am asked often about how Brandon (my former husband) and I separated the way we did. At some point I started recording various experiences and responses. I started writing what I know. While this is only a single individual's anecdote of divorce, with estimates of 33-43% of adults 20-64 years old "ever divorced," I have reason to hope and believe it's generalizable (Mayol-Garcia, Gurrentz, and Krieder 2021).

Plus, at the intersection of my own divorce, motherhood, and formal education (teaching in K-12 school settings for over 13 years and obtaining my master of education in psychology along the way), I became passionate about empowering parents to uncouple better, to support all domains of children's development through separation and divorce, to better navigate something as high stakes as co-parenting. While I never planned to pursue a path that would transform me into such a proponent of divorcing differently, here I find myself—adamantly advocating for the best and brightest potential outcomes for all family members affected by it. I really believe we, as a society, can both view and do divorce better.

Divorce

Divorce is a loaded word. For many, associations with it are pretty negative. The word alone often elicits unpleasant feelings, ranging from discomfort to disgust and beyond. Occasionally, I'll still get a pit in my stomach at the mention of divorce, likely left over from years of believing it was a very bad, cowardly, and selfish thing. However, the construct has undergone some major reprogramming in my core. Granted, it's taken years, but now I find myself grateful for divorce.

Because of divorce, I am friends with the father of my children; because of divorce, our kids have better relationships with both parents; because of divorce, my unconventional family is thriving. Divorce isn't a bad or sad or taboo thing in our world anymore. This book is an account of falling and rising through divorce, of burning down and rebuilding through divorce, of working so damn hard to *do divorce differently* and all that's been made possible because of that.

And please don't confuse anyone doing divorce differently, graciously even, with the idea that it must have been somehow easier or less complicated than your more common, messy and hostile divorce. I didn't know it was possible to hurt as much as I did and have; just recounting experiences in the chapters that follow stirred memories of such heartache that I'd often walk away from this project for months at a time. I'd return when I trusted I was in a headspace where I could sit with painful recollections, sit with difficult self-reflection, sit with heavy and heightened awareness, sit with simple acceptance of what is and isn't.

My divorce was hands-down the most gut-wrenching, chest-heavy hurt I've ever known and the hardest thing I've ever done. There was a lot of working through the bad and the ugly to get to the happy and authentic space my family occupies now. This book dives into both the how and the hard of reaching this space. It's a long game for sure. But I honestly believe that with intention, work, attempting to fix what and where you've messed up, learning from what can't be fixed, and constantly striving to believe in and practice more grace, gratitude, and abundance, divorce won't inevitably break a family, but instead release all members to heal and grow!

Intentions

Who is this book for? It's largely and selfishly for me. A lot of energy was moved through writing, a lot of hurt and joy processed, a lot learned. This book is for my kids. Part of me hopes they never care to read it. I picture them pursuing beautiful paths where of course they've long since and well-integrated their parents' divorce into their own stories. But, if they ever need additional evidence of how huge and unconditionally they are loved, that's in here. This book is for you, and whatever prompted you to pick it up.

If you have already made the difficult decision to divorce and are looking for a relatable account of someone navigating the delicate uncoupling and co-parenting balance during and afterward, I hope you find something of value here. And on that note, I want to share one of the most important, powerful, easy-to-say, next-to-impossible-to-implement practices I've come out the other side with here: set intentions (in line with core values) and make certain agreements with yourself right now, then work your ass off to honor them.

I have stood at more character crossroads over the past eight years than my entire life previously. I can think of countless instances where I chose grace and kindness, and countless others where I was defensive and cruel; plenty of both are outlined in this account. I am immeasurably grateful for Brandon, my former spouse and forever co-parenting partner. Even when we could hardly speak to each other without things either escalating fast or completely breaking down, we established certain intentions.

At the very beginning of our divorce journey—and wow if that isn't long and exhausting with infinite opportunities to turn mean and bitter—we set joint intentions to be as mature and reasonable adults as possible, to hit pause and walk away when "mature and reasonable" wasn't an option, to put our kids first, to protect them as much as we could, to filter our words and actions through the question, "How will this affect our family?" It has been over seven years since we first started the paperwork and process that would dissolve our marriage, and we continue to share these important intentions.

Crossroads

I also want to clarify what this book is not. It is not a book about if or when to get divorced. If you're currently feeling stuck or searching for direction at the impossible-seeming crossroads of *if* to get divorced, I have a hodgepodge of suggestions before we get too into my story. Really, these are applicable wherever you find yourself in the divorce decision and journey. Keep in mind, I explored these resources and/or implemented these ideas over years, not all at once. If you are hurting and feeling desperate for support with next steps, start with this first suggestion:

Pursue Professional Support

I revised this heading at least a dozen times from *Get Help* to *Consider Help* to *Obtain Support ASAP*. I certainly waited too long. Ultimately, I reached a state where I couldn't wait any longer. I needed some serious support and help to keep showing up for my kids, for myself, for my one life. I was past fragile and afraid that I would simply shatter into pieces at any more hurt. But through the seasons leading up to and of my divorce, there was always more hurt. There was another signature required at the courthouse, another difficult conversation with Brandon, another instance I didn't have the reserve to parent my three young kids with emotional intelligence, another night spent silently sobbing and wondering if we would all be okay.

I participated in a few consultations with various therapists and coaches before finding Kate Carson. Kate is an uncoupling coach based in Santa Barbara, California. My finding then working with Kate was arguably the most important thing I did for myself and my family through and following the whole divorce process. It was a big financial commitment for me, but it was an investment I understood—knew with every fragile piece of me—I couldn't afford *not* to make.

I used to be so uncomfortable at the thought, much less the practice, of putting myself first and pursuing the support I needed. I remember being irritated almost every time I'd fly. I don't love flying to begin with, then the flight attendants instruct me to secure my own oxygen mask first.

What the hell, Delta? I'd think. How sad and deep the conditioning runs to prioritize serving others, to put our needs last, and to stay small that this piece of sound safety advice could elicit a guilty feeling and defensive reaction. Not only is it okay, it is strong and brave to proactively obtain the help we need. Kate was my oxygen mask. I couldn't love and support my kids through their parents' divorce if I couldn't pick myself up off the bathroom floor.

I should have reached out sooner. Not that my marriage's outcome would have been different necessarily, but therapy/coaching fosters awareness, healing, goodwill, openness to change—all things I could have used more of earlier. If you're living in that limbo land of to stay or go, waffling between believing it's time to either fight for or flee from a marriage, trying to make sense of what exactly landed you at this crossroads to begin with, that's a lot for a heart to hold and a mind to process independently. Find a good-fit therapist or coach to help ground and guide you through such a turbulent chapter.

Pre- or post-divorce, no divorce, whatever your situation—I also agree with the sentiment that if you're a human, had a childhood, and live in a culture, you'll benefit from therapy. It's never too early or too late to pursue professional support.

Seek Out Resources That Educate, Inspire, and Empower

- *Conscious Uncoupling* (Thomas 2016). In part one of this book, Katherine Woodward Thomas discusses and validates the unbearable pain we feel when a core attachment is threatened, as well as what to try before deciding to uncouple. In part two, she outlines five steps for a conscious, kind uncoupling. Her work was instrumental in supporting me through some very confusing phases.

- Any and every Brené Brown book! *The Gifts of Imperfection* (2010) was a huge eye-opener that there were other ways to live; the idea of living more honestly, vulnerably, and authentically resonated. I was immediately and powerfully drawn to Dr. Brown's work.

I can't remember when I first read *Daring Greatly* (Brown 2012). I know it was before Brandon and I reached such a contentious place that we could hardly talk to each other about the state of our marriage without it getting ugly, and well before we stopped talking altogether.

I remember trying to share some impressions I had while reading it. We were driving past scenic reservoirs through our lovely neighborhood to our comfortable home while our three young kids slept in the backseat. My life was good, undeniably good enough. I should have been grateful; why was I feeling drowned in confusion and sadness?

After double-checking the kids were all still asleep, then staring back out my window, I brought up Teddy Roosevelt's "The Man in the Arena" speech (1910) that inspired the book's title, eventually whispering, "I think daring greatly in our lives would look like us getting divorced."

A year post-divorce, I would pick up *Rising Strong* (2017) and continue making sense of my story with the help of Brown's research and insight. You'll be better prepared to work through change and hardship with better perspective by familiarizing yourself with her work.

- *Tiny Beautiful Things* (Strayed 2012) and *Brave Enough* (Strayed 2015). So much wisdom in Cheryl Strayed's responses to other humans looking for guidance through their heaviest chapters. My dear friend, Susie, gifted me *Brave Enough*, a collection of Strayed's quotes, in the earliest stages of my divorce. (This memoir opens with a quote from that cherished book.)

I grew up believing I was supposed to read books of religious scripture. I struggled through the Book of Mormon and the Bible, always failing to find the wisdom or feel the peace others testified of, but I finally understood that elusive experience in the pages of *Brave Enough*. Now I gift this book to friends the way missionaries share their books of scripture. I've read it cover to cover more times than I can count and am so grateful Susie guessed it'd be comforting through my dark night of the soul.

- *Untamed* (Doyle 2020). This book was published years after my divorce was final, but it's fitting to recommend here because its message is empowering for anyone, in any situation, to return to themselves and relearn how to know things.

Ironically enough, I read Doyle's earlier novel, *Love Warrior* (2016), when I was still hoping to save my own marriage. I loved every page but was oddly unsurprised to reach the afterword and discover she and her husband had since ended their marriage. In that incredible and best-selling novel of her marriage's redemption, I sensed something between the lines, behind the words. Maybe one woman trying to ignore her own knowing can sense another's. *Untamed* is brilliant and will inspire you to find your knowing.

- Elizabeth Gilbert's words—written, spoken, quoted. Pick up *Eat, Pray, Love* (2007) or *Big Magic* (2016). Filter your podcast library to find her. There was one particular *On Being* episode where she spoke so honestly about the importance of joy in our lives, not to be confused with pleasure, but genuine joy (Tippett 2016). At a time when I was feeling very little, it was oddly hopeful. I felt compelled to choose the hard that'd ultimately return the joy.

"The most interesting moment of a person's life is what happens to them when all their certainties go away. Then who do you become? And then what do you look for? That's the moment when the universe is offering up an invitation, saying, 'Come and find me...'" (Gilbert, n.d.). Her words gave me new perspective and hope. Maybe faith and identity crises, horrible mistakes, and even divorce were part of the plan. What if all this pain, heartache, uncertainty, and challenging change wasn't failure, but instead (or at very least, also) an invitation?

- *Didn't See That Coming* (Hollis 2020). Another book not published until a couple years after my divorce, but with every page, I couldn't stop thinking how I would have clung to her words years ago. I'm specifically recommending it here because of how powerfully she articulates what *not* to do as a parent going through something difficult. It's so hugely important, and because I could never say it better, I'm including this crucial reminder:

  > Your kids are never old enough to watch you have a breakdown. Your kids are never, ever old enough for you—the parent—to process your pain, grief, fear, and anxieties with them. Never. It's not your child's job to hold space for you to fall apart. Call your therapist, your priest, your rabbi, or your best friend but don't you dare ask your kids to carry you through a hard season. It is your job to be strong for them, even if you have to fake it. That's what you signed up for. (128)

  Whatever the current state of your marriage, whatever the future holds, read and reread this, and act accordingly.

Find an Outlet to Process

Running and writing are my biggest outlets. Maybe for you it's baking, listening to podcasts, painting, rollerblading—whatever feels safe and helps you move energy. I've run countless miles with my thoughts, deepest fears, brightest hopes. I've written innumerable words, many of which are long since deleted or thrown away, but it's always helped me to move emotions/thoughts/experiences to text.

Get this: I even wrote to advice columnist and podcast host Dear Sugar (alias of my beloved Cheryl Strayed) around a year before officially separating, asking how one ever decides to end a marriage. I assumed she wouldn't be able to answer it; she probably wouldn't

WITH GRACE AND GRATITUDE

even see it, as there was nothing novel or unique in my question that would warrant the show's attention. Still, outlining my dilemma in an organized letter was helpful. And the response was validating:

Dear Brave Soul,

If you've written to us with a question, we thank you for entrusting us with your story. We're sorry we can't respond personally to most of the letters we receive, but please keep in mind something we say on the show all the time: there is power in the act of setting down your story. (Email message to Meg Campbell from Dear Sugar, 2017)

I sent that question already knowing the answer. I'd read plenty of Cheryl Strayed's responses to those stay-or-go questions. I could guess her answer would be what she'd been telling listeners all along: You don't need to look outside yourself; you need to get in touch with and listen to your core. Chances are the answer is there, but it's scary. Maybe it's not even a conscious knowing yet, but there's some awareness that finding and listening to what you already know is terrifying because it will ask a lot of you, it will require action, and taking ownership of that core knowing will change you.

I had asked friends, I had asked family, I had asked Google what I should do at this crossroads of if to get divorced…I finally asked Cheryl Strayed. Of course, Dear Sugar couldn't answer this for me, but the automatic reply's wisdom holds up. There is power in the endeavor of exploring and owning your story.

Understand Why We Stay

People stay in committed relationships out of love, duty, and/or structure. It's often some combination of the three. Some literature specifically explores remaining in or leaving relationships in the context of interpersonal commitment (dedication) and constraint commitments: perceived, material and felt (Rhoades, Stanley, and

Markman 2010). Perceived constraints include feeling social pressure to remain together, like pressure from extended family, religious values, community norms, etc. Material constraints would include co-owning resources, from furniture to cars to homes—everything that feels intimidating and overwhelming to divide weighs heavy on these stay-or-go decisions. Felt constraint is more abstract but refers to the sense of feeling stuck or trapped in a relationship.

Work to understand why you are staying or what's potentially driving you to go. Which direction feels most aligned with your core, with the wisest part of you? What can you live authentically with and what are you willing to risk or lose to get there? What is and isn't sustainable? What core values are you honoring and/or sacrificing in this relationship? Start exploring hard questions.

Choose YOU

Start the work of learning to value yourself, love yourself, prioritize yourself. Work on you. Learn to listen to you. All of this is way easier said than done, and arguably the all-important work of the human experience: meeting and loving ourselves, in the service of being able to fully and presently participate in this existence. (Hopefully, in doing so, we will come to know joy, lessen other's suffering, and leave our tiny corner of this planet better than we found it.)

Yet this meeting ourselves is sadly something many of us miss during formative years because we're busy checking all the boxes and attending to the countless "shoulds" presented to us at young ages; it's difficult to distinguish core versus conditioned wiring. It's scary but important work to table the boxes, to stop "shoulding" on yourself, to stop expecting anyone else to make you happy, fill voids, or give your life meaning. I am still and will always be working on this. But in the context of contemplating divorce, starting the soul work will serve to either improve and save your marriage or empower you to part ways.

I'm sitting on the edge of my bathtub, alone in my home, and on the phone with Kate Carson, my uncoupling coach. It's one of our earlier visits; I think I'm giving her important background information about my story. I share some about my upbringing, my history with Brandon, how I'm in the middle of a complicated divorce and so desperately need help. She listened, but at some point—I'm sure when my narrative was clearly leaning less factual and more trying to convince her of my victimhood—she stopped me, and in the most warm and wise voice said, "You can point fingers all day. You can point fingers at Brandon and what he could or should have done differently. You can point fingers at the church you've since left. You can point fingers at your parents, at your past. I am interested in the finger pointing back at you right now, understanding your role in all of this. I can help you with that."

Again, I found myself in the middle of one of those wreck-and-rescue wisdom moments. This is what I signed up for. Later I'd dive deeper into things like family of origin dynamics, attachment theory, core beliefs, and cognitive-behavioral techniques; but at the time, I needed tools to show up and move forward in the here and now. I didn't feel even the least bit defensive at hearing Kate call this out. I was so out of touch with myself, I was trying to make sense of my world falling apart through some external lens clouded with so much resentment, anger, and pain that I was ignoring my role in all of it. And that was the thing, the only thing, I had any control over addressing and hoping to better understand one day. At the crossroads of my divorce, the huge work before me was to find my core, the version of myself that I wanted to know and wanted my kids to know.

Disclaimer

Another important clarification is that nothing I share here, or possibly advise within the context of my own story, applies to abusive marriages or relationships. If you are in danger, get out, get safe, get help. Abusive partners do not deserve your patience through a conscious uncoupling; they aren't capable of one right now.

On the flipside of this, don't accuse abuse when/where that's truly not fair to your former partner. If you've reached the point of dissolving a marriage, chances are there's been emotional harm, neglect, borderline verbal abuse—plenty of hurt across the board (I realize it is sometimes more one-sided than others). I've seen couples start calling out all sorts of abuse endured once the decision is made to separate. It's easy to get incredibly nasty upon the reality of divorce setting in.

I'm not questioning another's experience; I'm encouraging any broken-feeling soul to get a therapist or coach. I'm encouraging you to pause in that space between stimulus and response. I'm encouraging you to work to uncouple in a manner that leaves you open to grow instead of small and mean and stuck.

We often need another's objective and regulated nervous system to help us process such immense pain, to help us create and maintain healthy boundaries, to support us in doing whatever it takes to not get tiny-hearted and cruel. The reason friends and family can't exclusively fill this role is because they love you dearly, they have a horse in this race, an emotional stake in your divorce. You can rely on them for countless other things but often need a trained professional to both validate your pain and call your bullshit.

I understand it asks so much impulse control of your frontal lobe to stay calm and grounded, to not say, claim, or accuse horrible things through divorce. Without time and space to regulate and reflect, those horrible and hurtful things you're desperate to accuse seem true-enough; it would feel right and vindicating to shout them in those lowest moments. But I can almost guarantee, a day will come when you are painfully aware of your conduct through this phase. Others, particularly your kids (if that applies), will have sharp and emotionally charged memories of this time as well. Hopefully that's powerful motivation to utilize any resources available to keep moving forward in line with core values of love, compassion, and collective healing.

PART 2

WHY

"Mom...Why?"

"Mom, why'd you and Dad get divorced?" The question came from my then-11-year-old son, Jude, seemingly out of nowhere while driving to a running practice. I was immediately flooded with feelings of confusion and guilt. It is wild how a handful of words, formed into a simple question and spoken out loud by my bright, beautiful son can momentarily transport me back to such a heavy and painful place. My mind was racing but making slow progress toward forming a response, competing with the concentration it took to appear calm and unshaken.

I'm no stranger to this practice, remaining straight-faced while breathing through internal panic. *What, what'd he just ask me? No, no, no. Why?!* It's not that I wasn't prepared for this question; there was a point I was beyond prepared for it. I'd been living in terrified anticipation of it for months. But that was over two years ago. Now it caught me completely off guard, and I wonder if my momentary shock was perceptible to Jude.

I finally responded, "That's a good question. We never gave you specific reasons, huh?"

"No, not really," he answered.

Did he sound sad? No, maybe? But he must be sad. Divorce is sad. Your parents not wanting to be married anymore is sad. He's gotta be sad. Thoughts and beliefs I'd been challenging for the past few years consumed my awareness, seeming determined that I finally accept their validity. I'm not sure why this felt like such a pivotal moment. I guess I was getting comfortable in my assumption we'd done divorce relatively well and were shaping the aftermath well. His dad and I were textbook conscious uncouplers; we were a healthy, high-functioning, unconventional family. What do I say to not undo any progress now?

I finally stumbled through the same talking points his dad and I agreed upon when we first told the kids our plan to divorce:

1. This (our decision to divorce) has nothing to do with you.
2. We love you, forever and unconditionally.
3. We will always be a family.

Jude was disappointed, probably hoping I'd forgotten this broken-record response. I am frustrated with my answer too. We are very open and honest with each other; the confliction I feel over how much or little to say right now is super uncomfortable.

"I'm sorry, babe. I know that's not what you were looking for. Please always talk to me, always ask questions; this is a difficult one for me too. I really believe that one day we will all make more sense of it, but right now I don't have a better answer."

We pulled into the parking lot. Jude was smiling now, singing along in his incredible voice to "Don't Stop Me Now" (one of his favorite Queen songs) after our conversation's unsatisfying end, characteristically back to enjoying the present. I looked over at him: my happy, music-loving, science-loving, easy-going, crazy-tough yet crazy-aware, wise-way-beyond-his-years oldest son.

"Love you big. Have fun," I said.

"Thanks, Mom. Love you too," he hollered, shutting the car door and heading inside.

Turning out of the parking lot, I put on my purple Goodr glasses and cried. Just a short hour ago, I would have claimed we were all largely adjusted to our new normal; it surprised me how this stung.

Strawberry

Two weeks after that conversation with Jude, I was trying to wrap my head around a lot of things. COVID-19 had reached Utah in the spring of 2020, and almost overnight our everyday lives looked very different. Schools had just closed, everything was getting canceled; we were reading and hearing about the devastation this novel virus was causing in other parts of the world, especially Italy, and wondering if the US was next. We collectively witnessed the principle of scarcity in action, unable to find toilet paper, hand sanitizer, or something as random as my favorite Highlander Grogg coffee anywhere. We'd all been instructed to practice social distancing and stay home as much as possible; there was a sense of ambiguous loss all around and a lot of unknowns. Able to recognize the magnitude and far-reaching consequences of this pandemic, I felt almost guilty that my little bubble was relatively unaffected. If anything, I appreciated the forced slowdown and was loving all the extra and unique time I had with my kids and close friends.

My pre-pandemic world of juggling working full-time, graduate school, and of course momming full-time (dang, if managing three kids' busy schedules isn't a lot), I had all but completely stopped my most important self-care practice. This mass closing gave me my mountain time back, if only for a brief season. I skinned (winter hiking up a mountain on skis with strips of grippy fabric stuck to the bases) and ran more in March and April of 2020 than I had in the previous six months combined. And I needed it.

At 30 years old, trail time got me through a pretty debilitating faith-turned-identity crisis, countless miles kept me grounded through the deepest heartache I'd ever known dissolving a marriage at 33–34, and it was on this early morning skin with dear friends at age 36 that I made sense of how to best support my kids in making their own sense of their parents' divorce.

Kari, Liza, and I were making our way up the Strawberry service road of our local Snowbasin ski resort. Between the sun rising on the east-facing slope we were climbing, the snow-covered mountains, and a thin cloud cover, the lighting was amazing—soft but sharp at the same time. We'd stopped to shed a layer of clothing, and now the temperature felt just right too. My gear is outdated and ridiculously heavy for uphill travel, but I couldn't care less. The fact that I wouldn't have money for many new or nice things after divorce was, fortunately, one of the easier realities for me to accept. (Other consequences, especially those forced on the kids due to their mom's reduced circumstances was a different story; something I still struggle with and address in more detail later.)

The company this Strawberry morning was outstanding. I sometimes assume that goes without saying, but I realize you may not know my friends. I sincerely hope you know people like them. I am incredibly lucky to have some amazing women in my life. Vulnerable, wise, kind, and brave women who intentionally choose to believe in abundance and practice authenticity. My girlfriends are total badasses, and I love them fiercely.

We moved at a good conversational pace, talking about the crazy world we were living in and all that'd changed so quickly due to COVID. No school due to COVID, no soccer or tumbling due to COVID. I actually made dinner this week due to COVID. We talked and laughed about the pros and cons of distance learning. You can either have a nice day or you can help your child with math, but you can't have/do both. We acknowledged the heaviness of it all, totally oblivious at the time that the worst was yet to come. We also all agreed this experience of being forced to slow down had thrown into sharp contrast just how "too busy" we had become.

From here the subject of how we're inevitably messing up our kids (10 kids between the three of us, ages 6–18) was brought up, with Kari expressing frustration over her teenage daughter borrowing her Lululemon leggings without asking. I wasn't necessarily planning to mention it but found myself confiding, "Jude asked me why Brandon and I got divorced." Not quite in line with Lulu-tight-taking, but it'd been weighing on me.

"I didn't know what to say," I continued. "I worry any answer I give, my kids will internalize in ways I don't anticipate or can't understand. I don't know how to explain constructs like romantic love and marriage when their young experience with and understanding of love is what they feel for their family, their friends, their pets." And on I went, always circling back to this nagging feeling that I owed Jude a better answer than the go-to responses I'd adopted from researching the dos and don'ts of how to talk to kids about divorce. Was it time to abandon those talking points? If so, I needed help replacing them. What do I tell him?

Liza is my almost-official therapist friend (if her MFT licensing exam hadn't been canceled due to COVID). Talk about someone who has found their calling in life! She said the most simple yet profound thing.

"Meg, you can't answer that for him. Any reasons you give would be your reasons, not his, and you are still trying to understand and make better sense of those yourself. You and Brandon may have a shared understanding of general reasons behind your divorce, but still, your individual experiences and reasons are different and unique. Your job isn't to give Jude answers, it's to help him find his own. Support him in trying to make sense of his experience; attempting to explain yours won't accomplish that."

I felt both relieved that I hadn't totally effed everything up in not answering Jude more directly the other day, and desperate for more Liza wisdom.

"How do I do that?" I pressed.

"Ask questions. Ask him to tell you more. See if he can articulate his experiences, thoughts, feelings. Ask him, 'What's it like having parents who are divorced? What's it like for you that Dad and I aren't married, but still good friends?' Then listen."

So…maybe Jude isn't sad; maybe he's a thoughtful and curious 11-year-old trying to make sense of a story?

We'd reached our uphill destination, removed the skins from the bases of our skis, and headed down. Skiing has always felt like magic, like peace, like home—certainly a core passion and core piece of my identity puzzle. This particular trip down the mountain, my world made more sense. I was able to throw my head back on a gradual section, breathe deep, and smile at the irony of a Brené Brown quote that filled my mind, one that's been taped to my bathroom mirror for years: "Owning our story can be hard, but not nearly as difficult as spending our lives running from it. Embracing our vulnerabilities is risky but not nearly as dangerous as giving up on love and belonging and joy—the experiences that make us the most vulnerable. Only when we are brave enough to explore the darkness will we discover the infinite power of our light" (2010, 6).

Story is our way home, and Jude was bravely exploring a confusing chapter of his own. My sweet kids don't need my narrative of the divorce; they need me to sit with them in the vulnerable space of trying to understand and integrate their experiences so they can embrace what is. As parents we want to protect our kids, but enabling them to ever run from or ignore their own dark chapters is a disservice. I resolved then and there to more actively support my kids in their attempts at owning, understanding, and integrating, even when it's uncomfortable and scary. We will feel it together, trusting we will know love, belonging, and joy.

Better This Way

"Remember when you asked me the other day why Dad and I got divorced, and I told you I didn't have an answer right now?" I asked Jude, after a day of processing Liza's comments and insight.

"Yeah."

"Would it be okay if I ask you something instead?"

"Sure," he replied, curious now.

"What's it like for you, having parents who are divorced?"

There was a long pause. It was next to impossible for me to not jump in and fill it, but I could see Jude was thinking. I'm quick to assume he's thinking sad and awful things about his parents' divorce, and I want so much to rescue him from these thoughts I've irrationally attributed, but instead I waited.

"I was sad at first, when you guys first told us...really sad...but I don't feel sad anymore." His tone is casual, totally unaware he's just said something so huge!

Hold up, what?! He doesn't feel sad. Jude doesn't feel sad over the divorce anymore. I could never have guessed at my reaction to that unsolicited statement. I divorced the father of my children, and he divorced me. No matter the varying circumstances surrounding a divorce, a choice to alter the family unit is impossibly scary. The guilt I'd internalized over the years from choosing divorce was in my bones, my blood, my being; it'd become such a deep-rooted part of me, I must have long forgotten its weight.

We know the analogy: a frog thrown into boiling water will jump right out, but when placed in room temperature water that is slowly brought to a boil, it will miss its window to escape. The years leading up to and of the divorce were emotionally exhausting and hard; my world felt like a roller coaster of survival mode, yet the guilt was constant and steady. If there had been a window where I could have effectively challenged or addressed it, I missed it. So, when Jude spoke those words, *I'm not sad anymore*, I was instantly lighter and filled with such unexpected hope. He was waking me up to new possibilities, new stories, new potential endings. And of course, this isn't to say he won't feel sadness over it ever again as he continues to integrate this fact of his life; but he didn't feel the same sadness that we didn't trust would ever pass years ago, and that was big.

"Why do you think that is?" I asked.

"I guess I didn't know what to expect. We were all so sad, and surprised. Dad was moving out and I didn't know what was going to happen. But I still see him a lot, and we still do stuff all together. And it kind of just seems like everything is better this way."

I thought Brandon and I had sheltered the kids from our marriage problems. We hid the external stuff; we didn't fight in front of them, didn't speak negatively of each other, didn't ever intentionally try to manipulate them into picking a side. But you can't fake the core and can't mask the energy that gives away what is true and real. Our kids are sponges, and their parents' struggling marriage weighed on them too, even if they weren't consciously aware of it. Jude saying, "It just seems better this way," was him articulating (in 11-year-old language) how we all felt: more authentic, lighter, living and being was easier this way.

Scary Questions

It took me three months to ask my two girls, Violet and Story, that same question. Of course, I wanted to support them in making sense of their experiences of their parents' separation, but I kept questioning my timing. They were younger. They were 7 and 4 years old at the time of our divorce, and 10 and 7 when I was contemplating this question-asking. I wondered if I should wait for them to bring it up. That was certainly the easiest option. But what if they never brought it up? What if they needed someone to model talking about difficult and uncomfortable things? I found myself stalling. Despite Jude surprising me in the best possible way with his response, I was still scared.

A seemingly random reminder reentered my awareness around this time, encouraging me to ask the scary questions. "If we don't have questions, there won't be any miracles for us. I don't know about you, but I need miracles in my life. I want miracles in my life. I hunger and thirst for miracles in my life. So I think I better ask questions— questions from the heart, questions that hurt, questions with answers that I'm afraid will hurt" (Okazaki 1998, 230).

Chieko Okazaki was a writer, educator, and religious leader. I found her teachings 16 years after her death, and ironically enough, at the height of my personal crisis of the same faith she embraced. I was drawn to her story; she valued education, obtaining numerous degrees herself, teaching in elementary schools, and eventually working in administration. Elementary school teachers are my people. I adore and appreciate them immensely; Okazaki's story naturally fascinated me.

I've spent a great deal of mental and emotional energy deliberating whether or not to include any of my history with organized religion in this account. Over years of writing and rounds of editing, I've gone back and forth—what to leave in and out remains far from obvious. I genuinely wish to be sensitive whenever referencing a faith tradition so deeply personal and important to people I love and respect. I realize, however, my experiences and perceptions (when it comes to religion) will seem the opposite, rather insensitive. I'm also aware of the possibility some readers will justify dismissing me as an "angry apostate," resulting in a missed opportunity to discuss divorcing differently, which is the whole point of this project. Ultimately, it's a risk I feel the need to take; the integrity of my divorce story is compromised if I were to try and leave religion out. So please bear with me through some pre-divorce churchy background.

There was a point in my adult life (early thirties) that I was furious with the Church of Jesus Christ of Latter-day Saints (a.k.a. the LDS church, a.k.a. Mormonism). The anger came after a long season of researching, studying, soul-searching, and asking hard questions. Upon finally determining the set of beliefs and faith traditions that I'd worked hard to embrace and practice my whole life weren't true, I felt inexcusably deceived and robbed of both precious time and life experience by this religion I'd belonged to for the past 30 years.

I struggled to reconcile many of Chieko Okazaki's teachings that resonated with what I knew of and observed happening in the present-day church organization. What I struggled to understand then, but time and space and work (always work) have brought some clarity—it wasn't my job to reconcile that. The path that wasn't working for me worked for her. The faith I was compelled to leave at 30 years old, she felt compelled to join at 15; I've come to honor instead of question or need to make sense of that. I'm instead grateful for her path, for her work and words that came before me, words that brought peace and made me brave.

Her words encouraged me to ask questions when other religious leaders promoted dismissing and shelving them. While the answers I found at this personal faith-wavering juncture broke my heart and infuriated me, they also liberated me—or rather gave me the courage to liberate myself. I would eventually leave and formally resign my membership from the LDS church—one of the most courageous things I'd ever done at the time, and remains a multigenerational trajectory-changing act I'm very proud of, all thanks to a willingness to ask and explore hard questions.

My exodus from that religion could comprise a whole other memoir, though I will address various parallels between it and my divorce throughout this book. I am no longer angry at or full of resentment toward the LDS church, and thankfully I'm far from feeling in any position to judge another's path. While still aware of harmful church practices and policies, I can also recognize and appreciate some of the positive influences and lessons that have stuck with me from my membership and trust the universe to remind me of those when needed. Jude's answer that he "wasn't sad anymore" was a miracle made possible not by any all-knowing, puppeteer god, but by questions.

Thoughts on Miracles

Besides, if there is a god responsible for miracles, this god is also responsible for tragedy, or at least responsible for not preventing tragedies with miracles. How finicky is that system?! Where was my young grandmother's cancer-curing miracle? She passed years before my birth. My most salient memory of her isn't of her but of my own young mother breaking down in the aisle of a grocery store, overcome by unexpected grief at the reminder her mom was gone—she was gone for the big things, like the birth of grandkids; and she was gone for the little things, for something as minor as a recipe question her daughter just realized she had never asked, and never would.

Not on par with life-saving miracles, but what about my marriage-saving miracle? Where was the miracle protecting my three kids from the adverse childhood experiences (ACEs) divorce delivered? ACEs are traumatic events experienced in childhood and highly correlated with negative adult health outcomes. While the experience of trauma is broad and subjective, research on ACEs has identified several experiences explicitly measured in determining an individual's ACEs score. "Were your parents ever separated or divorced? If yes, enter 1" (CDC, n.d.). The higher the ACEs score, the higher the likelihood domains of physical, mental, and emotional health are negatively impacted as adults. (Another fact I tortured myself with as a helping professional who chose divorce.)

People spend lifetimes trying to understand, chase, and be worthy of miracles, often living in fear of falling short and being dealt a tragic hand instead. I grew up believing my Mormon God heard and answered my prayers; no problem was too small to approach him with, even misplaced keys to a periwinkle Volkswagen Jetta. How convenient for me and my very privileged circumstances. Once I grew more aware of horrible injustice existing elsewhere, this was unacceptable. It felt wrong, nonsensical, and dangerous that some god was dishing out good fortune here and devastation there. I grew skeptical of this god and system, but trying to believe, because faithful members should, I evolved into a rather superstitious and fearful young adult.

In the middle of my own faith crisis, finally questioning this belief system at 30 years old, I hardly felt prepared to own any answers and choices for myself in the highly concentrated LDS community where we resided, much less ask my kids to deviate from the majority and norms. In hindsight, I can see more clearly how long it took and how hard I had to work to get out from under all that fear: fear of God, fear of church leaders, fear of friends' and neighbors' judgment. Thank the universe I somehow did because I went on to overhear hard questions and miraculous conversations between a couple of eight-year-old boys, like this:

Jude's friend: Are you Mormon?
Jude: No.
Friend: Do you go to a different church?
Jude: Nope.
Friend: So, you aren't Mormon and you don't go to church, but you believe in God, right?
Jude: I don't know.
Friend (shocked): What do you mean, you don't know?
Jude: How does anyone really know for sure, and which god? Whose god? Different religions believe in different gods, so I don't know.

Friend: Well, what do you believe in?
Jude (thinking for a minute): Love. I believe in love.

So simple. Was it always this simple? I couldn't have answered this myself 10 years ago, but now I'm with Jude (who I'm assuming—in that thinking minute—was recalling impactful conversations we've had since "quitting church"). I also believe in love, in the world-changing power of grace, gratitude, and presence. I believe in abundance and the resilience of the human spirit. I believe both amazing and awful things happen by chance. I believe other times we are responsible for the joy and heartache we experience. I believe questions and work are key to understanding our world, our relationships, ourselves, and how we want to spend our time here. The important questions, when explored, will prompt the work and change your life. *Do I believe in the religion I was born into? Are these faith traditions kind? Is this marriage honest/real/fulfilling? What if I leave this church? What if I got divorced? What are MY core values, am I honoring those?*

There's a Pool

Those once-intimidating questions about church membership later paled in comparison to questions about divorce. We survived leaving a religion—a decision that carried damning and eternal consequences if you accept LDS teachings of an afterlife—so it wasn't a decision I took lightly, nor was I able to make it free of others' intense concern and occasionally shame-evoking criticism. Still, as big as that felt to commit to and own at the time, it didn't quite prepare me for the terror that'd come with choosing divorce and how to help my kids field questions about it a few years later.

I absolutely hated the fact they'd need to answer for and explain something they didn't want and would have never chosen themselves. Brandon and I had already left them no say over their out-group, religious-minority membership—something they navigate daily. Whether it's my second grader being informed at recess that Jesus is sad she's not baptized or my middle schoolers sitting still as hands raise all around them at a school-wide assembly when the guest speaker asks, "Who here is LDS?"

Now we were insisting they also grow up with divorced parents; they'd stick out like sore thumbs in this conservative valley and have to answer for it. Questions about choices—especially those you know others perceive as poor—force you to own answers you may not totally trust yourself yet, and that's uncomfortable. It's why we're tempted to return to what's familiar through every step of big change; it's why questions about the change may be so triggering.

I suppose it shouldn't surprise me that kids typically address those "scary" questions rather competently. Young kids are more in touch with their intuition, their knowing, their sense of what's real and right, their core. Hard questions have never seemed to phase my own kids the way they did (still occasionally do) me. I like to believe it's because we haven't indoctrinated "right" answers in, haven't conditioned any core knowing out, haven't encouraged blind faith in anything they aren't cognitively developed enough to explore themselves, and we haven't used fear or shame to produce desired behavior or answers.

Like with the church membership questions, turns out I overestimated the awfulness of those divorce-related questions too. Eavesdropping on my then six-year-old daughter's weekend playdate, I overheard Story's friend ask her, "Where's your dad?" (My chest tightened, my stomach dropped, I felt sick that Story had been asked about his absence.)

"Probably at his apartment," she answered. (I didn't detect a trace of the panic I was feeling in her little voice.)

"What, where?"

"His apartment, where he lives."

"Your dad doesn't live here?! Why not?"

Story went on to answer her, as casual as could be. (I would have questioned if she was forcing the calm collectedness if she wasn't six and completely transparent.) "My parents are divorced. My dad lives at his apartment. There are bunk beds, and a pool!"

"Oh, cool," her friend replied. "Can we go swimming?"

All this to say I was scared of scary questions! I hesitated asking my girls about their parents' divorce because I was afraid the answers would hurt. And this was maxing out my metric for potentially scary answers. (So far the closest comparable was coming to difficult realizations about a church I'd sacrificed so much time, energy, money, and self-worth to—that was rough, but paled in comparison to the possibility I'd learn that I had hurt my babies with divorce.)

While that fear was real and terrifying, it was also silly when I thought logically about it. Violet and Story's responses and answers were there, somewhere. They lived through their parents' divorce, so of course they have memories, questions, thoughts, and feelings around it, regardless if we avoid speaking them aloud or not. That fear of painful answers was protecting me, not them. It was preventing me from holding and processing this shared-yet-unique experience with my sweet girls. *Ask the questions, even when you are afraid the answers will hurt. Ask the hard questions.*

Now my girls' answers weren't quite as miraculous as Jude's, or maybe they were more so, depending on perspective. Violet was sad I never slept over with them at Dad's apartment. Story was sad I never went to Logan with them (to visit Dad's side of the family) anymore. Both girls had sad memories of when we first told them about the divorce. Both were happy we still did stuff as a family but wished it was everything and all the time. They didn't volunteer any answers that validated our decision to divorce; if anything, their answers hurt more than not, but this wasn't about me. Maybe the miracle was talking about it together and them hopefully trusting that we can talk about hard things again and again, because hard things need processing again and again.

Here Goes...

Over the past few years, I've journaled some of my thoughts on two Instagram accounts: one completely private and one more of a family scrap/chatbook. I never intended to use these posts as a book outline when I first shared or recorded them, and while it's been difficult to not edit any in hindsight, they provide an honest look into my experience of divorce. Some chapters begin with these various posts; when that's the case, I have included the date originally shared. I reflect on these posts, as well as therapy notes and journal entries from the past five years, trying to give more context and add any insight that might be useful.

I also have a number of personal heroes I'll continue to mention/reference throughout this book—various authors, therapists, coaches, and friends. I've tried to include the work, examples, guidance, and wisdom that's proved most wreck-and-rescuing to me. Lastly, while Brandon declined to coauthor any of this account, I've done my best to represent his position and perceptions fairly based on conversations and questions I asked him in writing this.

Unless I obtained special permission, outside of myself, Brandon, and the professionals whose work I cite, all other names have been changed.

PART 3

2018

With Sadness and Hope

It is with both sadness and hope for future healing that Brandon and I want to let our family and friends know that we have dissolved our marriage. After nearly 14 years together, we have mutually decided that divorce is our next right step. We realize people will be curious as to why, and we worry excessively over how speculation and rumors will hurt our beautiful kids. In hoping this might spare them even a few difficult conversations, I am taking to social media to share a brief explanation.

In our preparing to "consciously uncouple," we've read a lot, learned a lot and grown so much already. We see no value in pointing fingers or assigning blame. The reasons anyone leaves a romantic relationship are often so personal and subjective; only the two souls who make up a union are qualified to know and decide when it's reached its end. Brandon and I are both forever grateful for all we've created, gained and learned from our time together. We are striving to be generous, kind and optimistic in the face of such loss. It is the death of a dream, but not without belief in a bright future for everyone on the other side. We aim to continue to choose kindness, goodness, authenticity, happiness and love; and we have no doubt our children will grow up whole. We will always be a family and forever refuse the adjective "broken" to describe us. Perhaps a non-traditional family, but always a family. Brandon and I anticipate remaining close friends, and are pretty damn determined to kill it at co-parenting.

We love Jude, Violet, and Story more than words can express; we would have done anything to spare them this experience if we weren't convinced we would all be better, healthier and happier for it one future someday. It is my most humble plea that, if you know our family, you not speak a negative word to our children about either of their parents, or the divorce. Brandon and I also ask that no one feels obligated to "take a side." We both wish to remain friends with all our mutual friends and maintain relationships with the other's extended family. We hope everyone touched by our separation (in some way or another) will continue to act civilly and with respect to all involved; please know our primary concern is that our kids are still accepted, shown big love, and not asked to answer for their parent's decision.

We have such newfound empathy for those who have navigated this path. It is anything but easy, and we wouldn't wish it on anyone. If you can authentically save your marriage for real and honest reasons, do. But if you can't (and it is not for anyone else to judge when and if a marriage can or should be salvaged), we've come to believe that divorce isn't this selfish, easy-out our culture has stigmatized it to be. At some point the scales tip and the terrifying realization hits that, for your family and situation, it is actually the most brave and vulnerable step forward.

At this crossroads, Brandon and I remain honored to forever share one of our lives' biggest and most beautiful dreams of raising children together. I can never thank Brandon enough for all that was given, all that he taught me, and for all the compassion with which we are now managing to release each other. We do not view this transition as a tragedy, but rather our family's next big adventure, and are embracing the fitting monkey bar analogy…So often in life "you have to let go at some point in order to move forward." So here is to trusting in all the beautiful, big, bright life ahead. Thanks for reading, supporting, and loving us.

—Brandon and Meg (@megbcampbell March 28, 2018)

Wow, the intense hell we'd been through leading up to the sharing of this announcement! How carefully Brandon and I navigated the very ugliest and darkest moments of our divorce journey is difficult for me to wrap my head around even now. Outside of a very select group of friends and family, this post was the first anyone in our circles heard about us separating.

Be selective in who you confide in and lean on during the earliest stages of uncoupling. You absolutely need your people, you need a support system (again, I highly recommend a trained professional as well), but be mindful of what you say and who you share with at your lowest points. Dissolving a marriage is heartbreaking; regardless of your reasons, this experience leaves you shattered and vulnerable. And while I wholeheartedly agree that vulnerability is courageous, Dr. Brené Brown highlights an important distinction between using vulnerability versus being vulnerable that's crucial to keep in mind here: "Oversharing is not vulnerability. In fact, it often results in disconnection, distrust, and disengagement...Using vulnerability is not the same thing as being vulnerable; it's the opposite—it's armor" (2012, 159-61). It's a given we're going to be extra tempted and especially susceptible to armor up through a divorce; try to recognize and challenge that defense mechanism. Armoring up, hurrying to spew your narrative, and oversharing will result in more pain.

Shera (a close friend, soul sister, masterful yoga instructor, and one of the most talented interior designers you'll ever meet) has a helpful analogy. Know your bedroom friends. Bedroom friends are simply *your people*, those allowed in your metaphorical bedroom. Picture your home/apartment/living space. Now picture others coming to visit. There are some you see coming and scramble out of line of sight while whisper-shouting at everyone home, "Don't answer the door!" And you all pretend no one's home until the uninvited visitor retreats. Then there are acquaintances who remain on the front porch where you engage in small talk. Closer friends are welcome in your living room and at your dining room table; you're invested in and appreciate these relationships, but they're still more surface level. Very few people are welcome in your bedroom, where you're the most vulnerable, where you may be found crying on the closet floor, where the armor comes off and expectations set down.

With divorce, you or your former spouse are both metaphorically and literally moving out of your once-shared bedroom. You owe each other and your family the courtesy of not talking about this on the porch. From the moment Brandon and I decided to divorce, move forward with the paperwork and officially file, to the afternoon we sat down with our kids to tell them, it was of the utmost importance to us that we protect them from painful rumors, that they not learn about their parents' divorce from someone or somewhere else. In our case this was a little over three months. Those three months were pure hell. Impossibly lonely and hard, and there were times I wanted to shout for the whole world to hear how mad and hurt and angry I was. But these were my adult emotions, the result of adult decisions, and it was not the time or place (because it is never the time or place) to ask my kids to witness or hold my rage.

I realize this timeline will look different for every situation. In homes where kids have observed hostility and fighting, talking to them earlier may make more sense. Other families may have the means to support one partner moving out before paperwork is even started. (Our three months had a lot to do with needing to refinance the home in my name so Brandon could use the cash-out we'd agree to split to move elsewhere. There were many pieces we couldn't expedite.) Regardless of varying circumstances, divorce is deeply personal. While it may be tempting to overshare on the porch or in your living room, try to trust that your future self, former partner, and kids will all thank you for being cognizant of who has earned a place in your bedroom.

So instead of gossiping or drinking or chasing equally broken guys (because the craziest and dumbest of distractions are tempting down in the lowest of lows), I needed some coping strategies. I talked to Kate (my uncoupling coach), I ran for many hours alone with my thoughts, I relied on bedroom friends and family, I read many a self-help book, I practiced meditating, and I threw myself into my kids' worlds and lives. They were hands-down my biggest motivation to handle each moment with as much compassion and emotional intelligence as I could manage. I was not in a place where I could trust myself to be strong, kind, mature, and to do the right things simply because they were the right things. But I always wanted to work toward the version of me I wanted for the mom of my kids.

Be kind with yourself when you screw up because you inevitably will. I did and still do and have to remind myself to embrace the growth mindset I incessantly preach to my own kids and students: you can grow your brain like you can grow your muscles, you can notice and redirect thoughts, you can shape your behavior and new ways of responding with work and practice. Growth and learning and healing will involve slipups; it's to be expected, especially with something as life-changing and delicate as divorce. To simply care about not perpetuating more hurt while experiencing deep emotional pain yourself is admirable, and hopefully motivation to keep going, keep trying, keep learning.

Wrong and Rightness

> Believe in the integrity and value of the jagged path. We don't always do the right thing on our way to rightness. (Strayed 2015, 25)

After years of living in limbo land (hard to stay, harder to go), Brandon and I first began filing for a divorce in January of 2017. In February of that year, I remember sobbing hysterically, begging Brandon to please go skiing with me instead of to our mediation appointment, to please give it—give us—a little more time. He eventually (though reluctantly) agreed. We canceled our mediation appointment, went skiing, and made our first appointment with a marriage therapist instead. What transpired the remainder of that year is another story entirely, comprising much of those beginning sections I'm not yet writing; indeed, the most jagged and darkest chapter of my life. A lot of wrong turns and missteps were taken on our way to rightness. Ultimately, it was too little, much too late for Brandon and me to repair or save our marriage. In January of 2018, we finished filing for divorce online, requesting to waive Utah's 90-day waiting period, and we were legally uncoupled on March 16, 2018.

I agonized over how and when we should tell the kids. At first, we thought we would wait until May, the end of the school year, because the thought of my older two having to return to school after we dropped this bomb made me want to throw up. But really, all of it made me want to throw up. Drawing on what I knew of childhood development and how well I knew my own kids, I would haunt myself with various scenarios, guessing at how they might react.

My youngest was in preschool. I knew Story's young age would lend itself to handling this change better than the rest of us. But I also knew she would grow up with very few, if any, memories of her parents married. She'd watch her older siblings devastated at the news, but would she come to resent the extra time they had in a traditional family? Heavy sigh.

Violet, my middle and intense child, would be instantly heartbroken and overwhelmed with sadness at the news. I wondered compulsively over how I'd comfort her, much less convince her that anything will ever feel okay again. Heavy sigh.

And Jude. He would take this hard and spend the most time in his own head trying to make sense of it. How would I reassure him that his parents are adults who made an adult decision, that this had nothing to do with him? Heavy sigh.

The closer we got to needing to tell the kids, the more I was tempted to talk myself into staying married for them. There were innumerable moments I was 100 percent ready to cancel the divorce to just forever avoid having to break this awful news. I had rationalized for a long time that it'd be better for Brandon and me to try and fake it till we make it married because a divorce would crush the kids. I understood they will experience hurt and heartache in their lives, was never naive to that inevitability, but choosing to be the cause of it was too much. For many years divorce wasn't an option, divorce was selfish, divorce wasn't fair to the kids.

Brandon occupied this same limbo land; it's why we waffled at that stay-or-go intersection for years. One of us would resolve to move forward with divorce, only to be talked out of it by the other. We'd taken the divorce education classes, read how important it is to stay if you can make it work, to stay if the kids don't see the conflict, to stay if there is no abuse. We took turns feeling crazy, awful, selfish, and silly for contemplating divorce at all.

Thankfully, we never completely settled into this dysfunctional dance, as my head filled with more questions. Where is the research on what staying does to the two souls who make up that kind of union and their kids living within it? That research doesn't exist, we don't know exactly who all is doing that, staying solely for the kids. (I think it's likely a lot.) Even though those outcomes aren't systematically studied, I felt safe in my assumption they aren't ideal. What if our kids need honest, whole parents more than they need married, broken ones? What if our kids never get to know the brightest versions of their parents because their parents convinced themselves that shrinking to fit in a convenient box of "traditional family" was better for the family? What if our kids never saw authentic living and loving because we decided instead to fake it for their sake? What if it wasn't divorce itself that hurt kids, but *how* parents divorced that mattered?

I did take comfort in other and extensive research I was familiar with. While there are various labels in the literature, parenting styles fall into four main categories: authoritative, permissive, uninvolved, and authoritarian. It's well documented and understood that authoritative parenting styles result in the best parent-child relationships and increase the chances of raising healthy, well-adjusted kids. Authoritative parents have high (but reasonable and loving) expectations, clear standards and boundaries, and are assertive, kind, and clear in their communication with kids. They're democratic, flexible, responsive, warm, and they allow their kids important learning opportunities through empathy and consequences.

If key characteristics of authoritative parenting include high warmth, high involvement, and high monitoring, what if we made it a priority to remain warm, involved, and aware? What if parents resolved to remain loving and stable presences in their kids' lives, to practice authoritative parenting through a divorce? Wouldn't that be a huge protective factor for kids?

While these questions always felt pressing and real and important, for years I continued convincing myself that, in our case, Brandon and I remaining married surely must be better for the kids. The kids, the kids, the kids. Fear of the unknown was so huge and heavy in me, I wasn't sleeping or eating well. I'd wake up wishing so desperately all of this had just been a bad dream, but day in and day out I'd wake up to the disappointing reality that my marriage was over, and we needed to tell our kids.

•◦●●●━━━━━━●━━━━━●●◦•

Certain things will always be a mystery when it comes to our particular love and why it grows or dies. But one thing is clear to me now:

There never was any possibility of my ex-wife and me making things work for our kids' sake.

Kids have so much power and magic and sway. But one thing they cannot do, and should never ever be expected to do, is to place the sparking defibrillators on mom and dad's busted love.

And by staying together for the sake of our kids, well, that is exactly what we would have been asking them to do. Their mother and I would have hammered away at the dam of our marriage until the whole thing just burst and drowned them in a raging flood of impossibility. See, in order for a marriage to work, or any relationship really, there has to be hardcore love, no? The unshakable galaxy of love you have for your own kids can't be substituted for the grown-up kind.

When two people say, 'Let's make this work for the kids,' they're already heading down the wrong path. In our case, had we used our kids as a main reason…or let's be honest…as an excuse to stay together. Oh, we would have been held in high regard by the family-values people and probably by at least half the world's religions, but the whole thing would have been the freakin' Sham of Shams. The love/the passion/the intense longing to remain together deep down in the marrow caves of our bones—none of that was present any more.

All we were after a decade of marriage and kids and confusion and sadness was two locust shells waiting for the wind to blow us away. No kid was ever gonna change that for us.

You can work on your marriage until the sun burns out, man. You can dig and dig in the rubble trying so hard to discover what has been lost. But if you don't ever find true love down under all that dirt and mangled past, then you need to ask yourself some real hard questions. You can maybe find love again even after you've both lost your way. But it has to be because that's what you both really want for each other, not the kids.

That's just the way it is. (Bielanko 2015)

More wreck-and-rescue wisdom. I stumbled across this article by Serge Bielanko in my researching should-we-stay-together-for-the-kids phase. That phase lasted for over two years, so I read plenty. Of all the resources I came across in that time, I saved the stuff that spoke to my soul. This article powerfully challenged my resolve to stay married for the kids. (I recommend anyone feeling that stay-for-the-kids guilt, go read it in its entirety.) I returned for any reassurance I could pull from these words as we got closer to the divorce talk.

Of the various things I know and guess and simply wonder at— and very few things fall under that "know" category—I *know* Brandon and I are healthier and happier individuals now than when we were married six-plus years ago. If we had stayed married, it would have been for our kids. While I like to think we'd never have come to resent them, or they us for putting them in that position, that is expecting the unfeasible—kids cannot salvage a marriage whose well-being was never their responsibility to begin with. When it felt impossible to trust any direction while deciding to divorce, I had to trust that staying married for the kids was unfair to our family.

Thoughts Become Things

The unknowns and what-ifs that occupied my mind those months leading up to telling the kids were terrifying. I knew I couldn't spend too much time in this fear; it wasn't serving anyone—not me and certainly not the people I was wildly trying to protect. I had to learn to be flexible and still during a time I was more desperate than ever for some control and answers. *Am I ruining my kids' lives? Will they be okay? How long until they are okay again? How will I ever find the words?*

Kate reminded me then, just as Liza reminded me later, that kids are their own autonomous beings. I have some influence over how they integrate their parents' divorce into their stories, but it's not solely my work to do. *My parents got divorced when I was nine...when I was seven...when I was four.* Those will be their new realities, new truths to hold. I only have control over how I carry and conduct myself right now. I can choose to be present, to validate their pain, to sit in the heavy with them, to attempt to help process their experience of this, to grieve and heal together, and—super importantly—I can do everything in my power to ensure I don't ask them to feel responsible for me, for my raw feelings toward their dad, for my adult pain.

I had to constantly remind myself this was the brave and honest step forward. It wasn't until much later I came to actually believe it, but thoughts become things. I embraced and repeated the thoughts, words, and information that resonated as true. *Will we do this now or later? This is honest and important. We will be okay. We will heal. Ready is a decision.*

Preparing for "The Talk"

I avoided writing about this part for a while. Even when you think you can tell your kids anything, within age-appropriate parameters of course, even if you trust that clear, honest, and real communication has already been established as a priority and practice within the family, I can't imagine anyone ever feeling prepared for this talk. Telling your kids their parents are getting divorced is unspeakably hard, yet you have to speak the words and own the content; it's the worst.

My wise sister Erika—also one of my best friends, confidant, and go-to person for just about everything for as long as I can remember (I was 18 months old when she was born)—now also a skilled licensed clinical social worker by profession, had recommended the book *Talking to Your Kids about Divorce* (McBride 2016). I devoured the general chapters and those specific to my kids' ages. After lots of additional researching, reading, consulting with Kate, and talking with Brandon, we agreed it was best to tell our kids two weeks before he was planning to move out. We wanted to balance this timing and not just spring it on them, like, "We're getting divorced and Dad's moving out tomorrow" versus the other extreme of the kids knowing about our plan to separate before papers are even filed and having to live in a heavy middle space of sad anticipation.

Again, I recognize how incredibly lucky I was to have a co-parent willing to entertain this kind of discussion, then honor our joint plan. I realize we are a minority and I do not take that for granted. I understand others truly don't have the luxury of making such a plan. I also know most will claim they don't, regardless of the reality. I am (rather regularly) approached and asked how Brandon and I did and are doing this, collaborating and co-parenting so civilly. Most people are either amazed and complimentary or super skeptical. We've heard countless comments along the lines of:

"You guys are the exception…"

"Yeah, right…"

"Well, you're lucky _____ didn't happen, making that kind of divorce and co-parenting relationship impossible," and they fill in the blank with whatever personal reason they've used to justify throwing civility out the window through a breakup. To these comments I want to scream bullshit. Living through divorce, watching friends and acquaintances negotiate divorce, reading just about everything I could and can find on the subject, I am convinced that most any divorce has the potential to go either way: impressively gracious, horrifically messy, and everywhere in between. We were no exception.

I've mentioned there was plenty of dark and ugly stuff I'm not going to detail here; that's not the point of this account. Or, on the other hand, perhaps it's exactly the point—we purposefully and intentionally navigated that hell privately. We didn't broadcast, blame, and point fingers then. There is no point in doing so now. But I can assure you, with any dissolution of a once-primary relationship will come many and major reasons to turn absolutely awful. I can't even articulate how unfathomably difficult it was to live in line with that intention of uncoupling respectfully and protecting our kids day in and day out for months through the thick of our divorce. But we somehow did because we were the adults, we were the ones who created our current circumstances, and we were also the ones who accepted the major responsibility of prioritizing the physical, emotional, mental, and spiritual health of the beautiful beings we brought into this world.

To any super discouraged soul reading this right now feeling overwhelmed at that responsibility and that there's no end in sight—I know that space. May you feel some hope and find some resolve to uncouple differently, consciously, graciously. It is hard, harder than there are enough words for me to capture the magnitude of in these pages; but every beautiful, worthwhile, life-changing endeavor is made up of countless small, consistent, intentional actions over time. It does get easier, one step at a time, one breath to the next, remembering "Nothing ever happened in the past; it happened in the Now. Nothing will ever happen in the future; it will happen in the Now" (Tolle 2021). Stay present, stay focused on your goal of a gracious uncoupling, stay both strong and soft, and simply do whatever needs doing now.

In addition to just trying to trust some hippy-woo-woo-sounding reassurance (I get it), it also helped me to understand why things will/ do get easier from a neurophysiological perspective. "Neurons that fire together, wire together." Neuropsychologist Donald Hebb (1949) coined this catchy phrase decades ago, explaining how pathways in the brain are established and reinforced through repetition. As you intentionally practice responding consciously and with emotional intelligence at every bridge that divorce requires you to cross, it will get easier to continue responding that way. This also explains how/why individuals that do step down that uglier, messier divorce path often end up with ugly, messy divorce stories and legacies. It becomes easier and more natural to repeat thought and behavior patterns with every repetition; it's how habits are established, and habits shape your life. The whole idea of "watering what you want to grow;" do that with your ideal divorce conduct.

Even when Brandon and I could hardly stand to look at each other, we managed to agree on key co-parenting guidelines, all based around that joint intention of protecting our kids and our family:

- We'd tell the kids of our divorce together and present a united message, despite the two of us feeling anything but united. Kids deserve as much stability and consistency as possible through this news that will shatter the world as they know it.

- The kids would not hear us speak negatively about their other parent. Regardless of how hurt or furious we felt by/with each other, we'd remember, "That is the mom/dad of my kids." This requires a great deal of imagination and perspective taking! While my feelings toward Brandon were incredibly complicated and raw, I could never deny that my kids adored their dad, and it would pain them to hear me speak poorly of him. (Not sure if all states require the same or similar divorce education classes, but Utah mandated we complete two, one specific to parents of minor children. I opted to participate asynchronously and still clearly remember one video, analogizing the cognitive stress of divorce on kids to their physical inability to hold more weight than their young bodies are able. I watched an animated figure of a child literally crushed under the weight of a barbell, labeled divorce, they were attempting to hold overhead. Additional weights representing various parental behaviors, like bad-mouthing the other parent in front of or to kids, were added to the barbell, further straining the child trying to hold cognitive and emotional weight they're simply not capable of supporting.) There were days on end when Brandon and I didn't speak and very minimally communicated about the kids via text; if we did open our mouths (out of earshot of the kids), only cruel things came out, but neither of us ever questioned or attacked the other's love for the kids and our kids' love for both of us. I'll repeat, kids should never be expected to hold the adult pain that comes with ending a romantic relationship—sounds obvious but takes a TON of awareness and work to ensure we don't ask them to.

- Agree on what "reasons" behind the divorce decision you'll share. This will depend on the ages of your kids. There is a lot of literature on this subject; I suggest starting with *Talking to Your Kids about Divorce* and be mindful of separating your individual and personally perceived reasons with the reasons your children need in order to try and process what's happening. Brandon and I decided we needed our young kids to hear (and hopefully understand) three important things; those same things I repeated to Jude years later:

  ○ *We love you so much, nothing will ever change that.* Be prepared to not just remind them often, but be able to show them, to hold them through the talk and the weeks and months that follow. The love we have for our kids is deep, huge, and powerful. It is enough to reassure them through the biggest heartache their family has known if parents can decide they need their kids to feel their collective love more than they need to be individually right or vindicated. (This has been said a number of different times and ways: "Love your kids more than you hate your ex." I dislike the word *hate* and the label *ex* here, but the message holds up.)

  ○ *Divorce is a choice moms and dads make. It has nothing to do with you.* Now, both Brandon and I knew the part about it having nothing to do with kids wasn't completely true. In the sense that we wanted to model what honest and brave living and loving looked like for

53

our kids—how we'd decided the bigger tragedy wouldn't be our kids growing up with divorced parents, but growing up confused about what genuine romantic love looks like—where we worried over and were helpless to guess at what kind of energy they were absorbing and messages they were internalizing as a result of their parents' struggling marriage. In many ways, the divorce had a lot to do with the kids. But that kind of reasoning is for adult brains with an understanding of adult love. That reasoning wouldn't help their young minds and hearts understand why their dad was moving out or why their parents didn't want to be married to one another. I trust they will come to realize and understand those more mature reasons someday. But in the here and now of 9, 7, and 4 years old, they needed to hear and believe, "This has nothing to do with you." Kids are likely to fill in gaps and make up their own stories about the why. *Why'd my parents get divorced?* We need to actively block reasoning that'd result in them taking on any responsibility or questioning if it's their fault.

o   *We will always be a family. Our family will look different than it has, but parents never divorce kids, we're still and forever a family.* One more attempt to hopefully prevent a dangerous misunderstanding. Divorce is a choice parents make, but parents don't divorce kids. It's easy to forget the need to mention this because it so clearly goes without saying for most; but it's not that big of a jump for young minds to make. *If Mom and Dad are leaving each other, will they ever leave me too?* Reassure your kids over and over and over again that you are a family and no one is leaving them.

If it is the case that one parent is in fact leaving the family—rehab, jail, checking out, taking off—I'm truly sorry. I can only imagine how lonely that must feel. You, however, can still share similar and important messaging that you aren't going anywhere. Give your kids space and permission to still love the parent who has left without offering or instilling false hope they'll return. Their absence will be something you all unpack and work to make sense of for probably the rest of your lives, to some extent. With every new phase of life often comes a new need to reintegrate past experiences and trauma; sounds intense, and is intense—but healthier than burying and perma-running from it. Sending so much love to these families!

The Talk

It was the Friday before spring break, March of 2018. I can't remember if we actually called it a family meeting or the kids just started referring to that talk as a family meeting after the fact. Either way, we all developed some negative associations with the label "family meeting" and have yet to hold a second one. After a couple of years, however, we did start joking about family meetings and teasing, "who's getting divorced?" (Certainly took a hot minute, but I'm glad we're able to reference it now with a lightness made possible by the healing that's transpired since.)

My memory of "the talk" resides as an odd contradiction in my mind—painfully sharp, yet blurred, I think by the deep despair it was stored with. Of course the divorce changed me, but this talk specifically changed me. I know pain and suffering are transformative, but never have I experienced it so instant and irreversible. I went into this talk not knowing the level of sorrow I would experience during and right after it existed. Sounds dramatic, I know. My kids have beautiful, bright, and privileged lives. There are many and far worse things than your parents' amicable divorce. But I'm their mom, I'm supposed to protect them; instead, I was bringing devastating news, heartache, and permanent change. I could survive breaking my own heart; breaking my kids' was a different story. It was one of those intersections where I could no longer go on as I was. It was either crumble under the weight of all the heartbreak then and there or channel some reserve, conjure up some version of me able to occupy this terrifying space.

I sat down on the couch, almost frozen with fear and the worst anticipation I've ever known. The kids were curious, a little anxious. They knew something was up. I can't breathe, but I will myself to not cry, not yet.

No turning back, be brave, be strong. (Now, I can't recall verbatim what was shared, but some variation of the following.) "We love you all so, so much…bigger than the universe." Our kids start asking what's wrong. "You know how we talk about trusting and following your core? That is what Dad and I are trying to do now. This has been something we've thought and talked a lot about and feel is what's best for our family. We've decided to get divorced."

It's silent for only a matter of seconds; the kids waiting for us to take it back, rescue them from having to accept what was just shared. Then all three burst into tears, escalating quickly to hysterical sobs. My own vision blurs. I can hear Violet screaming "why" over and over in a voice I'd never heard before, but I can still hear it now like it was yesterday. I wonder where in my mind that auditory memory lives to always be retrieved so vividly. I swallow the thickest lump in my throat. I watch my babies completely come apart. I've never hated myself and Brandon more than I do in this moment. We caused this, we did this, and I was positive that nothing would be or feel okay ever again. Of course, I was wrong. At the time I even had some awareness and tools to know better, but it didn't matter. In this space where time seemed to stand still, I couldn't feel my hands; I felt out of my own body, only aware that my kids were deeply hurting, that I was party to choosing this, and that nothing was remotely okay.

Brandon and I are holding their sobbing, shaking bodies. We are crying with them now, but quietly, almost calmly despite the horrible, debilitating hurt. Our tears are validating their pain, our family's collective loss; but breaking down in front of our kids wasn't an option, and we were determined to get through those must-tell-them points. "This is a decision we made together. It has absolutely nothing to do with you. We will always, always be a family. We love you."

I don't know how long we sat in the living room or how many times we repeated some variation of those three things. *We love you… divorce has nothing to do with you…we will always be a family.* It felt like an eternity before Jude would meet my eyes. Violet asking questions in that same tone, raw with emotion and panic. Story's initial and innocent confusion, looking to her siblings and knowing this news was really bad. I'd long since stopped praying to the god of my childhood, but found myself silently pleading with the universe…*Please let them be okay, please help them through this, please let them feel joy again. I'm so sorry.*

"Spring break is officially ruined," Story declared, having decided that's one thing she's sure of among all the unknowns. This elicits tearful smiles from everyone, and I laugh softly at her painfully accurate understatement. I pull the kids closer, my love and need for them to be okay is overwhelming. I feel their pain in my soul. There is no unknowing this hurt; everything's changed.

Feel Every Step

I ran my first 50-mile trail ultramarathon in the spring of 2017. I'd be running around beautiful Bryce Canyon, a unique area of the southern Utah desert famous for the countless sandstone hoodoos formed by the weathering processes of frost wedging, wind and rain. This weekend would be extra unique with record high temperatures for that early in the year. It no joke felt like 50 miles on the surface of the sun. Any recency bias toward that race has long passed, and I still recall it being hellishly hot and miserable. Chatting with other runners on the trail, the question often came up, "Have you ran a fifty before?" Fellow runners expressed deep sympathy and concern upon learning that it was my first, commenting that I couldn't have picked worse conditions if I tried. I'd smile and think, *no shit.*

Wild and irrational thoughts would consume me for miles, like if I got through this I'd never go outside again, or I'd become nocturnal and only recreate outdoors when the sun was on the opposite side of the Earth, or I would start listening to my dermatologist and buy full body bathing suits because clearly the sun was evil! Around mile 30, I started hearing hopeful whispers of a stream crossing at mile 38. No one, though, could confirm or deny this stream's existence in June of 2017. All I could gather was some years it was running, others it was dry. How was I supposed to manage my expectations?!

People were dropping like flies. I'd later learn the county used its year's search and rescue budget in a single day extracting runners from this blistering course. As I neared mile 38, I was running near a man who looked even more miserable than I felt. He was obsessed with the idea of this stream. Every corner we'd round and not see it, he'd either shout or sigh (depending on how out of breath he was), "Fuuuuuuck!" *Can people die of disappointment?* I wondered silently. I was worried this guy might snap.

Luckily, we came to a low but running stream at mile 38.5. I spent a good 10 minutes rolling around in it like the happiest dog ever, very tempted to stay until the sun set. Thanks to some encouragement from Brandon, who joined me for the last 16 miles, I managed to drag myself out of that stream and eventually to the finish line. I finished many hours later than I had hoped and planned, and I'm no stranger to post-race disappointment, but that didn't even come this time. I had finished my first ultramarathon in extremely difficult conditions. It absolutely sucked. Sheer stubbornness is all that kept me going. I felt every step of that stupid, hot, hard race, after which, "feel every step" became an affirmation of sorts. What a gift, really, for a mind and body able to experience and feel every step of each run, each day—from the beautiful ones that take your breath away, to the heartbreaking ones that turn your world upside down.

Back in my living room and wrapping up "the talk," Brandon let our kids know he'll be moving out in two weeks and asks if we want to go see his apartment. We make the 20-minute drive together and walk around his soon-to-be-new apartment complex. Jude, Violet, and Story are constantly looking to us, trying to learn how to occupy this brand-new and foreign world that is our family's new reality. I still feel outside my body, determined to protect the kids while my own nervous system was scrambling trying to decide what protecting me looked like. I felt constantly on the verge of fight, flight, or freeze, but I would see my kids' nervous and wondering eyes, breathe through the panic and bring myself back to that moment.

I meet their eyes, I ask them how they feel about bunk beds, what they think of the pool, who's going to help Dad decorate. I'm not overly optimistic, I'm not trying to blanket all the heaviness with obnoxious positivity, and I'm not trying to convince the kids that we're all okay right now. I hope, though, that I'm showing them I believe we will be okay, that we can do hard things, and that we have each other. I feel every step and it is all of the sudden absolutely laughable to me that I ever thought something like Bryce Canyon 50 was painful.

Selfishness, Self-Care, Self-Compassion

> You might feel that loving yourself first and foremost is selfish, but it's the direct opposite. Because we're all connected, all part of the *same* consciousness, when we love ourselves fully and deeply, that love overflows and everybody wins. (Moorjani 2020)

It is oftentimes (and unfortunately) common to view divorce as a selfish decision to begin with, tempting some to view prioritizing self-care through divorce especially unwarranted. We need to redefine or destigmatize (or both) what the label "selfish" entails. I've started acknowledging at least two kinds, comprising ends of some selfish scale or continuum. There's asshat-selfish on one end, and authentic-selfish on the other. (Oh-so-creative labels, I know, but stick with me.) One big distinction involves how asshat-selfish people operate from a place of scarcity and need to feed their ego, while authentic-selfish people embrace abundance, understand the importance of boundaries with themselves and others, recognize there will be mistakes and the need for amends, but are striving to shape the wisest, kindest, most self-actualized versions of themselves. I have certainly been both asshat- and authentic-selfish in my 39 years.

I'm well aware that asshats are responsible for many a divorce. I also have an idea of how frequently divorce is the result of authentic-selfish people trying to be honest and brave. Whatever your reasons for uncoupling, regardless if you are the one leaving, being left, or it was a mutual decision, everyone loses when someone abandons themself. Find your most important and fulfilling self-care and self-love practices and prioritize these even when it feels impossible; you need to cultivate safe spaces through the whirlwind of divorce.

In addition to practicing self-care, something that's talked about less (but is equally important) is practicing self-compassion. In the past when I would feel unsure of myself or make mistakes, my natural response was to feel embarrassment and shame, to replay the failure over in my mind, engage in negative self-talk, question and/or criticize myself until I felt downright miserable. It wasn't until I started familiarizing myself with Dr. Kristin Neff's work (self-compassion.org) that I grew more aware of just how unfamiliar I was with this valuable skill.

Dr. Neff (n.d.) has identified three important elements of self-compassion, outlined as dichotomies: self-kindness versus self-judgment, common humanity versus isolation, and mindfulness versus overidentification. Self-kindness entails being warm and gentle with ourselves instead of harsh and critical. Understanding common humanity means we understand failure, hardship, and pain are universal truths of the human experience. If we ever find ourselves thinking we are the biggest screwups or completely singled out in our suffering, that's simply inaccurate, distorted thinking. And mindfulness allows us to feel, hold, and move emotions—the good, the bad, and the really rough stuff. We understand strong emotions will come and go, we can get curious about our emotions instead of being controlled by or making ourselves wrong for them, and we recognize that difficult emotions are part of even the happiest lives, so we are able to avoid over-identifying with them.

I finally feel like I have a decent handle on the common humanity and mindfulness aspects, but dang, that self-kindness versus self-judgment is a hard habit to first break then reestablish oppositely. Of my three kids, Violet is the most like me when it comes to certain perfectionist tendencies, having high expectations for herself and then being highly self-critical any time she even perceives she's fallen short. Perfectionism is the opposite of self-compassion, by the way; insisting on perfection from yourself is not only unreasonable, but rather cruel. So, I got passionate about intentionally practicing self-compassion out of wanting that habit and practice for my daughter.

It's neither of our defaults, but we are working on it. While I've routinely encouraged my kids to write down values, affirmations, and goal statements, I can't express the immense joy and relief I felt to pick up what I thought to be a piece of scrap paper in Violet's room and turn it over to find she'd started recording self-compassion statements as well:

> I am human.
> Everyone makes mistakes.
> I can try again.
> It's not the end of the world if I mess up.
> I'm important, valuable, and loved no matter what.

She acknowledged it's not what she'd naturally tell herself when she's messed up or is feeling disappointed. She wrote these statements down and started routinely practicing, so hopefully when she needs that self-compassion, she can access it. Violet was 12 at the time of this exchange; the thought that she gets to spend the rest of her life being kinder to herself, that one day it may even become the norm, brings me to the happiest of tears. I want this for her, for Story, for Jude, for their dad, for myself, for everyone. I want to see everyone win.

Firsts

> The sense of belonging I've always felt in the mountains feels so real to me it's almost tangible, and also arguably the biggest constant of my life. I suppose it's natural that I returned to them when I felt my sense of self unraveling...As I started hiking and trail running again, I quickly noticed that, even at my lowest points, I never failed to find hope and feel peace on the trails. They didn't care if I didn't have my shit together, they didn't get uncomfortable if I sobbed in their presence, they didn't get impatient with my questions, they didn't judge me for not having all, or sometimes any, of the answers. (Campbell 2017)

I wrote this in 2015 during that faith/identity crisis. It was published two years later by *Trail Sisters,* and to this day I still find and feel that sense of home in the mountains. Trail running in the mountains or desert is where I feel full of energy and alive, while also very calm and content. It's grounding and invigorating, exhausting and renewing, and has always felt like where I most easily and obviously belong. I had my first child in 2008, and over the next seven years had all but completely abandoned this hobby. As a young mom, I couldn't find enough hours in the day, wasn't getting enough sleep at night, and still believed it was selfish to leave my kids for something like running.

That belief slowly shifted over the next decade, and by second grade Jude brought home a Mother's Day trivia card that read: *What's something your mom always says?* Jude's response, recorded by his little hands in the most endearing writing: "I'm going for a run." I face-palmed and chuckled, hoping he actually hears things like, "*I love you...I'm so proud of you...Listening to your music makes me happy...Skiing with you is my favorite...*" even more. I acknowledged the mom guilt trying to take hold, then instead focused on the fact my eight-year-old recognized his mom participating in self-care. Luckily, I had found my way back to regular running by the time I was getting divorced; I can't even guess at the number of miles I spent on the trail those years, much less at the mental and emotional stability it enhanced.

It was in April of 2018 that I was scheduled to spend my first weekend without the kids. People had warned me that the first year post-divorce is hard, and it is—insanely hard. (It's not a coincidence the 2018 section of this memoir, my first year divorced, is significantly longer than the others.) All the firsts make for near-constant uncertainty; the newness is exhausting. The Monday before that weekend I was scheduled to spend alone, I started to freak out. What was I going to do? The house would be so quiet, yet my aching for the kids so loud and inescapable. The anticipated stillness, loneliness and restlessness felt suffocating. I needed to go run—something big, something bucket-list big.

I'd only be postponing that first weekend home alone, and not even by much, but this was the very thing I'd once been willing to stay married indefinitely to avoid. Choosing to get divorced meant less time with my kids; I struggled reconciling that choice with how much I don't want to miss a precious moment of their young lives. I had an idea of how quick 18 years will come and go, and choosing to miss any of it because of divorce felt inexcusable.

It would be a while before the guilt subsided, as I slowly began to understand the huge importance of quality over quantity when it comes to time with kids. I was scared to give up the amount. I wanted my kids with me always, but when you're in the thick of it, you can't always see how an unhappy marriage affects and weighs on the quality of every relationship in that family. Months later I would be able to recognize that choosing divorce made more authentic, honest, and open connections with my kids possible. But at the time, I had no way of knowing that understanding would come, and for this first weekend alone, I needed to be distracted on my feet, moving my body and working on something I'd be happy to accomplish.

Metrics

The Zion Traverse was incredible! Kolob Canyon to the East Rim entrance, self-supported 50 miles and then back home… lovely day! (@megbcampbell April 30, 2018)

How the stars aligned for four busy moms to pull off this Zion Traverse with only a couple days' notice I have no idea, but I am dang grateful it happened! In under 36 hours, we drove the five hours down to Wildcat Canyon (in Zion National Park, Utah), where we delivered food and water to a trailhead along the route that we'd need to support the next day's long effort. (Unable to carry all we'd need to eat and drink for 50 miles from the start, we identified a strategic drop spot. This was around mile 23 of the route and the only place we'd be able to refuel and refill water before reaching the Zion Grotto, a popular trailhead and picnic area in Zion Canyon, at around mile 39 of our traverse.) After dropping supplies, we stopped at a yummy burger joint in Virgin, Utah, where I enjoyed the best egg, bacon, avocado cheeseburger ever, before backtracking to our hotel in Cedar City.

We slept for about four hours before it was time to get up, get ready, and head back to the Kolob Canyon park entrance. Still half asleep, I dressed slowly while checking the weather one last time, debating how many extra clothing layers I wanted to stuff into my running pack. I shoved my small first aid kit and solar blanket as deep as I could, tempted to remove them in favor of a lighter pack, knowing, though, I wouldn't. For the amount of precision planning that goes into these adventures, responsible planning includes understanding that things can go wrong, and the plan may change, so I always haul around the minimal amount of gear that would allow me to survive a night outside.

I proceeded to fill up my water bags—a two-liter bladder for the back sleeve of my running vest, two smaller bags that fit into pockets on each side of the front straps. (I've referred to these as "boob bags" ever since I bought my very first running pack. They rest on my chest with nipples just inches from my face. Staying hydrated while running has never been more convenient.) I smile to myself, remembering the first family hike Jude was all of the sudden old enough to be amused at the nickname while refusing water from my "boob bags," requesting his own hydration pack for future hikes.

I added my bag of bacon, string cheese, peanut M&M's, salt pills, and apple sauce squeezes to my pack, then Googled coffee shops. Not sure why I thought anything would be open so early. Nothing near us was open until 5AM, and we'd be half an hour into our run by then. The thought of the next 12 hours and 50 miles with no coffee was stressful, felt irresponsible even. I could guess at the drowsiness, the fog, the headache that was sure to ensue. How had I not thought ahead here? (Yikes, I'm addicted to coffee.) Perhaps needless to say, I'd never been more relieved to see hotel lobby coffee ready so early. I filled up two cups for the road and we were on our way.

This run was stunning; talk about an incredible national park to traverse. While I remember it fondly, I also remember feeling rather numb; didn't exactly *feel every step* of this one. I hadn't run this distance since that hotter-than-hell Bryce Canyon 50-miler a year ago. I should have been more nervous, kept expecting to feel a healthy fear of this traverse knowing I was undertrained, but it never came. It was somewhere around mile 40, having just descended over 3,100 feet off the West Rim, now climbing out of the bottom of the canyon toward the East Rim, when I realized I was experiencing pain and discomfort differently than in the past. Even the intense heat beating down on us as we ascended the shadeless switchbacks up toward the East Rim wasn't irritating me like it normally would. The events of the past year had changed my perception of pain. I understood early in the whole divorce process that I was changed, that there was no unknowing some hurt; but this was my first opportunity to acknowledge it had, as cliché as it sounds, also made me stronger.

Even when we thought we were mere yards from the car at the East Rim trailhead (because numerous watches in our group were inaccurately reading 50 miles, probably from signals bouncing around canyon walls), only to consult a map and realize we still had five more to go. With every inch of my body just aching, an unexpected 5 more miles after 45 behind me was discouraging, but not remotely as hard as taking off my wedding ring for the last time.

Or starting my period at mile 47 without a tampon or liner or anything. Not too surprising that my period surprised me again. How I've gone so many years, month after month, never keeping track of when to expect my next one, I don't know. It's like those doctors' questionnaires asking, "Date of last menstruation." I always wonder who even knows that information.

Luckily, my friends (always more prepared than me) had packed extra tampons, and I couldn't care less about my bloody shorts. This inconvenience was ridiculously minor compared to filing divorce paperwork, refinancing a house to split the equity, deciding how many nights a year the kids would sleep at their dad's, working hard to regulate my nervous system and not lose my shit day in and day out through the scariest transition of my life. This was only the beginning of me realizing the many metrics divorce had altered, and to my surprise, some for the better.

Fear

> It takes courage to endure the sharp pains of self-discovery rather than choose to take the dull pain of unconsciousness that would last the rest of our lives…You are either on the path of love, or the path of fear. (Williamson 1992)

> I was—and still am—in awe of how powerful fear is. Its ability to both protect and sabotage us. I'd unintentionally embraced a fear-based decision-making model for most of my adult life. I was so accustomed to its presence, I didn't necessarily recognize the ever-present underlying fear influencing big decisions. (@runwriteheal June 10, 2018)

Fear and shame and not-good-enough conditioning runs deep. We're all exposed to it, some more systematically than others. In my case, I can't avoid attributing this largely to the LDS faith tradition I grew up in. I learned to fear God, to doubt my doubts, to doubt and fear others who questioned or wavered in their belief. At 29 years old, my world turned upside down when Brandon chose to leave the faith I was still practicing and planning to raise our kids in. I was devastated to learn that my then-husband was one of those others: a disbeliever, a quitter, an apostate.

I understand this may sound outrageous to those not familiar with the faith, and not wanting to dive too deep into Mormon doctrine, what's important to understand here is that when Brandon resigned his membership from the church, the consequences I still believed in were massive and heartbreaking. He was sent a letter from the First Presidency (the highest governing body of the LDS church) explaining all his covenants (agreements with God) were null and void, including his celestial marriage to me. Essentially, based on my understanding of the church's doctrine, his decision cost me my exaltation and eternal family—my promise of an afterlife in the highest degree of heaven with those I love most was gone. Like me, many close family, friends, and members of the community wholly believed my personal exaltation was compromised; the pity was palpable. This was a huge betrayal and a big freaking deal at the time.

I went to seek counsel from the bishop I was assigned to when my husband left the faith back in 2013. I was a distraught wife and worried mom of two young children, with another on the way. The bishop greeted me with a kind smile at his office door, we shook hands as I entered and then took a seat. The bishop sat opposite me, his desk between us, a picture of the Savior hanging above. The atmosphere felt dark and dreary. Our church building was old with brown hues, red brick, and yellow light, but it wasn't the colors or outdated design that made me uncomfortable in this space.

I'd never felt at ease sitting opposite a bishop. I think this is largely because I grew up participating in "worthiness interviews." (I've heard such interviews have been scrutinized and the LDS church forced to revise the format more recently, but throughout my childhood and adolescence these visits involved me meeting alone with a man who was given great power over me by way of his calling as Bishop. He was granted permission by a church organization to ask me wildly inappropriate questions about my thoughts, beliefs, and behaviors.

These questions ranged from whether I believed Joseph Smith to be the founding prophet of our church to if I ever had impure sexual thoughts, and further still, if I ever acted on them.) While this visit wasn't a worthiness interview and this bishop had never himself asked me those questions, my nervous system still distrusted the dynamic. I only showed up because I believed my family's eternal salvation was in jeopardy.

"Jude and Violet are sealed to you, but this baby will be born outside of the covenant." I listened, seven months pregnant with Story, choking back tears as my then-bishop (someone I quite literally believed to be a mouthpiece of God on Earth at the time) explained the consequences of Brandon's decision. (In Mormonism, "sealing" refers to the union of a man, woman, and any children they have for time and all eternity. Sealing is considered a sacred ordinance that is performed only in LDS temples by men who hold the Melchizedek Priesthood—the power and authority of God here on Earth. Members of the LDS faith believe, as I did in this meeting, that being sealed to your family in this life ensures you are together in the next.)

"What do you mean? What about this baby?" I pressed, hugging my round belly, incredibly distraught.

"This is my first experience with any member voluntarily resigning their membership and forfeiting covenants. I have had to look into the ramifications more myself. You and Brandon remain civilly married, but not eternally. Jude and Violet will remain sealed to you because they were born under the covenant of your Celestial marriage; however, that's not the case with this baby," my bishop explained.

My heart rate increases, I grow nauseous. I clasp my hands together to try and calm their shaking, I'm utterly dumbfounded.

"Can I just be sealed to her after she's born?"

"I'm afraid not," he answered and seemed hesitant to go on. This bishop was a good man, raised in the same system I was, blindly believing the same truths and convinced he was doing good serving in this church leadership capacity.

What we both understood, but he was being careful not to explicitly say, was this: *I'm afraid not. You are a woman and therefore do not hold the proper keys to single-handedly ensure your child is with you in the afterlife. While we have assured you that being a wife and mother are your greatest earthly callings, you have no actual voice or power in this organization. Your eternal salvation has and will always depend on a man.*

He continued, "In order for this baby to be sealed to you, you would need to divorce Brandon and be sealed to a worthy priesthood holder. Then all of your children would be sealed to you under that covenant. I'm so sorry."

I was speechless. For the past year I'd been either stubbornly refusing to talk to Brandon about his reasons for leaving or arguing with and blaming him for "ruining our eternal family." Now, however, I found myself wondering, *What if he's right?* I'd been so busy clinging to my fear and self-righteous judgment of Brandon, believing he was both weak and cruel to explore his doubts instead of shelving them like the rest of us. But now what? Before I could suppress the fear or turn off the doubt, I was asking myself hard questions: *What god wants to break up families? What middleman has the power to decide any relationship I earn with my child here is severed in the next life because of a decision made by her dad? What organization would suggest you are divinely justified to divorce/disown/distance yourself from family members pursuing a different path? What god cares more about good standing in his church than love?* Whatever I still believed, it wasn't what this bishop just described.

•••••————————•————————••••

I ultimately explored those hard questions further and am grateful that Brandon and I did not get divorced over his decision to leave the LDS church. We attempted to navigate a mixed-faith marriage for some time before I too requested my name be removed from all membership records three years later. Still, the dots between us leaving the Mormon church and our divorce are not difficult to connect. In leaving the church—a particularly strict one at that, with warnings of a dire fate when abandoned—we learned to choose courage over comfort, authenticity over convenience, and faith in ourselves over fear. Denouncing what many friends and family still adamantly believed, choosing to marginalize ourselves and our kids in a county with an active LDS majority, and pursuing the unknown was scary. We knew what a Mormon life looked like, that lens was comfortable, the worldview familiar. We could only guess at what our post-Mormon experience would entail—we had no map for this road less traveled.

There wasn't excessive compassion or understanding from my previous tribe on my way out. I understood their disappointment, their sadness, and their concern because I'd been them. Their treatment of me was my treatment of Brandon during his exodus, years ahead of me. Even when he tried to explain this was a decision his integrity demanded, I wouldn't hear it. How lonely that must have been for him. And how sad that I'd let a religious organization convince me to value what it claimed was true over actual people, over my husband. I had been afraid, and fear tends to drown out empathy while fueling judgment. To acknowledge that others may be pursuing an equally valuable path is to admit the one and only path you've devoted your life to is not the one and only path. Much like leaving the church, dissolving a marriage includes more admissions of many hard truths.

I've had a few years now to explore the parallels between leaving the church and getting divorced. The potential of being wrong when so much is at stake is often too much to entertain; I wouldn't and didn't for a long time. It's powerfully tempting to operate under sunk cost fallacies: *I've been a member of the church my whole life. I've been with my partner for 14 years. I should stick it out. There's so much time, energy, and experience invested, so much shared history.* Sharing kids makes this particular fallacy extra powerful and terrifying to challenge, and the dissonance builds.

Cognitive dissonance refers to the psychological stress we experience upon encountering information that contradicts our beliefs, our routines, our way of life. (Like a church leader explaining your third child will not be joining you in the afterlife, or questioning if staying married for the kids is a viable plan, or holding your sobbing children after the announcement that their dad is moving out.) This dissonance is uncomfortable and scary; we're naturally inclined to not acknowledge or explore anything that challenges our safe and familiar status quo. But cognitive dissonance is important, ideally serving to broaden our understanding and enlighten us.

It's a beautiful, valuable skill to be able and willing to adjust beliefs, perceptions, and practices in light of new information. It was thanks to my faith crisis that I really learned to sit with cognitive dissonance, with fear, with uncertainty—all things I'd be sitting with, heavier than ever, once I began to understand and accept my marriage was ending.

The path of love involves challenging those fallacies, embracing the dissonance, getting curious instead of hustling to escape or avoid it. Listen to what those observed incongruencies are trying to tell you, be open to actions they may ask, then hopefully and eventually, act. Wish I could say the fear and dissonance subsides with the divorce decree; I suppose mindfully addressing it is simply another practice that gets easier with each repetition. And it's those repetitions, those choices to continually and consistently choose the path of love over fear, that will shape your success story.

Umbrellas

We had this Lake Powell trip planned since pre-divorce. We go with our good friends and the kids love it. Brandon and I agreed we'd all still go; the kids would have been so disappointed if we canceled, or one parent stayed home. I am beyond lucky to have a co-parent who has agreed and made great effort to uncouple peacefully so that still taking this vacation together was even an option.

I've decided my favorite thing about boating (since I struggle with almost every activity that involves being pulled behind a boat) are the boat snuggles with kids—the best! Toward the end of the trip, and to my huge surprise, Jude commented that he thought I had more fun this year than last, that he noticed I smiled and laughed more.

Swimming from the boat to a sunny piece of slick rock, my close friend mentioned that Brandon seemed to be doing better, happier, and more engaged. I agreed. Our divorce was

final exactly and only three months ago today. I have learned
so much in that time; definitely have come to understand that
being alone and being lonely are two very different things.
(@runwriteheal June 16, 2018)

Years ago, I came across a painting portraying a line of people, all
but one hunched below a dark umbrella under a dark sky. With the
exception of that one individual, the others' steps appear forced, sad,
and heavy. In sharp contrast to the mostly grayscale painting is a
small section of light and color, illuminating that lone figure who has
closed their umbrella and looked up, only to realize it wasn't raining
or dark and dreary at all. A straightforward but powerful analogy and
image that's stuck with me. This was my experience losing and leaving
a religion. I'd been handed an umbrella at such a young age, it was
difficult to question and ultimately close it, but the light on the other
side of fundamentalism was brighter and more liberating than I could
have ever guessed.

Living in an unhappy/inauthentic marriage is kind of like living
under an umbrella. You think it's good for you, it's protecting your
family, and you're responsible and a good parent to keep it up. Life
under the umbrella is good enough, and after all, it's what you should
want. Reaching a point where you wonder if the brave next step is
to possibly close it is scary as hell. You feel inexcusably selfish, your
head swims with those fallacies and aches from the dissonance because
you've lived under it "just fine" for so long.

But if/when you do close it, pay attention to how you feel in the
months that follow. It will likely be the wildest roller coaster of highs
and lows; your vocabulary will be forced to expand for new emotions
your previous labels just don't fit as your whole body aches to hold
them. But just maybe, if you can feel and process and work to take each
next step with grace, gratitude, intention, and heart—maybe, amidst
all of the unknown you feel lighter, more honest. You survived closing
the umbrella, and in looking up, your beautiful son comments that
you're smiling and laughing more. A good friend notices your kids'

father is happier and more present. You trust for the first time in a long time that things will be okay, even better this way.

While still under the umbrella, I feared I'd be so lonely on the other side, but once out from under it, I understood with deep clarity that lonely is what Brandon and I were for many years. Now I was alone in the sense that I was recently divorced and newly single, but I wasn't lonely; I was moving toward myself.

The Core

> You can't fake the core. The truth that lives there will eventually win out. It's a god we must obey, a force that brings us all inevitably to our knees. It asks, eternally: *Will you do it later or will you do it now?* (Strayed 2015, 84)

> Loneliness is driven by a lack of authenticity. High levels of true belonging results from showing up in your life. (Brown quoted in Tippetts 2018)

> Ready is a decision, not a feeling. (A theme that's resurfaced often, been discussed in many a therapy/coaching session—no idea where I first heard it.)

I saved and contemplated these truth bombs a little obsessively through the season of and after my divorce. Think I'd known in my core we needed to get divorced for some time. As much as I cared about my husband, cherished the life we built together, loved our family...you can't fake the core, and trying to fight or deny it leads to a range of sad and unhealthy outcomes. I've alluded to the significant period of time before our divorce (on the scale of years) where we waffled between ambivalence, anger, depression, resentment, and intense loneliness... feeling more and more lost every day. Yet I never once felt ready to leave, ready to start the paperwork, ready to actually get divorced. I'm not sure anyone ever feels ready to dissolve a marriage. It took actually closing the umbrella to finally believe and trust it was the right decision, but this doesn't mean I automatically knew how to live without it.

Be patient with yourself in navigating all the unknown that follows the dissolution of a primary attachment. It takes time to learn to stand alone, to learn to belong to yourself. You can know divorce was the right thing, but you can't skip grieving the loss. You can feel relieved and absolutely devastated at the same time. Those years that followed were a huge exercise in holding both: fear and hope, joy and sadness, trust and skepticism, hurting and healing. I remember feeling so very tired. Trying to find a whole new normal at 35 years old and desperate to not mess up my kids too badly in the process was exhausting. Be gentle with yourself, drink water, get enough sleep, go on adventures, cry on the bathroom floor…break down and rebuild over and over again. With as much grace and gratitude as you can muster, trust your process.

Choose Your Hard

> Breakfast at Jenny Lake Lodge this morning, which, by the way, is crazy fancy! When my phone tells me there's a restaurant two miles away and we're all hungry, it never crossed my mind we could be so out of place showing up at a lodge in the Tetons in hiking clothes. I kept telling the kids, "Please have good manners, please have good manners."
>
> Then this afternoon…There is no panic like the panic of realizing you may miss the last ferry across Jenny Lake with three tired kids and Violet whining at you, "Ugh, why do you have to love mountains?!" These three hiked 13 tough miles today, running the last one to catch the ferry. Crazy proud of them. (@megbcampbell July 6, 2018)

I wanted to document being proud of my kids on this Grand Teton National Park trip, which I was and am, but remembering this trip now, I'm proud of myself! Looking at the pictures, my kids were little: Jude was 9, Violet and Story had just turned 8 and 5, respectively. I reserved a teepee yurt pretty last minute, packed our hiking gear and bear spray, and we were Teton-bound.

Traveling alone with my kids wasn't new. We had visited the Grand Canyon, Bryce Canyon National Park, Crested Butte, Colorado, my parents in California, my sister in Northern Idaho pre-divorce on occasions when Brandon was unable to join us. But this first trip, officially divorced, was different. Planning it was different, being there was different, coming home was different. It took a minute to understand what and why it all felt so foreign.

A quick Google search will tell you the top five most stressful life events include:

- Death of a loved one
- Major illness or injury
- Divorce
- Job loss
- Moving

Divorce is big. It was the biggest and scariest decision I ever made, then the aftermath isn't any less scary or stressful, at least not at first. This trip was different from any other I'd previously taken alone with the kids because I couldn't resent Brandon for not being there or blame him for anything that might go wrong. I felt a great deal of responsibility, which is a good thing. I was hiking three young kids through no-joke mountains, but it was much bigger than just this weekend. Moving forward, I was responsible for myself, my future hopes and plans, my relationships with my kids, and what I did with the rest of this one life.

I have a complicated relationship with Ayn Rand's work, spanning at least a decade. While the philosophy of objectivism resonates on many levels, I also take issue with various limitations, particularly its feeling void of gratitude while promoting individualism, seemingly at the expense of connection and compassion. Nevertheless, words that I'd read numerous times before filled my head with new meaning this weekend: "I swear, by my life and my love of it, that I will never live for the sake of another, nor ask another to live for mine" (Rand 1957, 1069).

75

Many couples fall into an unhealthy practice of living for each other, or at least believing their partner is responsible for their quality of life and overall happiness. I used to romanticize the crap out of this idea; many of us are conditioned to. We want to believe in fairy tales, soul mates, true love, and happily ever after. But those ideas lead to unreasonable expectations, and those expectations set marriages up to crash and burn. Fairytale-influenced expectations are objectively harmful to relationships if/when they suggest happiness is found in another. It was a novel concept to come across in my thirties that we are responsible for our own happiness. Connection is important and relationships are important; others can enhance our happiness, but they should never be responsible for it. I certainly didn't understand or believe this when I was married. I felt Brandon was equally, if not more so, responsible for my happiness, and I resented him for everything I didn't like about myself and my life. How wild and backwards!

If partners find they are able to support each other in pursuit of their highest actualized selves while never taking ownership of the other's journey, well, I imagine that is what being both held and free feels like. Sounds simple, but we know it's not. Brandon and I weren't able to understand or accept this in the context of our marriage; divorce gifted us that. Sometimes you can repair and remodel relationships; I've seen a handful of couples do it beautifully. Other times you have to burn it to the ground and rebuild independently. Marriage is hard, divorce is hard, repairing is hard, rebuilding is hard…

Choose your hard.

Cascade Canyon

> Motherfuckitude…Love this concept from Cheryl Strayed.
> Run, write, parent, live, learn, breakdown, rebuild and love
> like a mother-fucker. (@runwriteheal July 8, 2018)

I recorded this gem of a caption on my completely private Instagram account below the image of a lone, asymmetrical pine tree. (Aware that many followers of my family account wouldn't appreciate the language,

I saved it in my private little corner of the internet, because this concept and picture captured our Jackson trip so beautifully—incredibly hard and amazing!) The tree's top was singed charcoal black from a lightning strike, still standing tall and owning its space alongside rugged cliffs, a raging river, countless other trees in much better shape, wildflowers blanketing the ground beneath it—exuding motherfuckitude.

About five miles into our hike up Cascade Canyon, Story fell asleep in my arms, where she stayed for the next hour until I could no longer feel my hands. My shoulders ached under the weight of my day pack, heavy with water, food, and extra layers for the four of us. All day I'd been on high alert for any sign of moose and bears. Trying to keep the kids fueled, hydrated, and semi-entertained (or at least distracted) enough to continue putting one foot in front of the other for hours on end is always a big job. And I irresponsibly didn't plan for just how much our average pace would slow on the return, which is why I ended up begging and bribing everyone to run to catch the last ferry across Jenny Lake and back to our car. I was exhausted, and it was hard, but I'd choose it again and again.

While this weekend adventure was pretty spontaneous, there was nothing random about where we headed. Jackson has always been a happy bubble place, the Tetons always magical. I remember pulling into the Heart Six Ranch in Moran, Wyoming. The kids were thrilled to spot the teepees, while I was wondering why it didn't cross my mind that maybe I should have found some accommodations with a locking door for my first post-divorce, solo-parent trip. Oh well. The sight of my three beautiful kids, full of joy and giddy-excited, running around against the backdrop of those peaks, I knew the trip was a good thing. Choose the hard that also feels like home, or as Glennon Doyle (2020) says, "the right kind of hard"; then tackle it with some motherfuckitude (Strayed 2015), over and over again.

Overthinking

Every few years I'll cut and donate my hair. Sometimes I wish I could follow it, see where it's ended up; I'm sure the stories of wig recipients would absolutely break my heart. The practice always serves as a reminder of how prone I am to take my good health totally for granted. It's also become this odd/random way of measuring time. I remember the inches I graduated college and got married with, the inches that saw Jude and Violet born, the inches that grew alongside Story in my belly. As I look at this donation, I can't help but think of all that's changed. Plenty of symbolism today, and/or I just overthink most things. (@megbcampbell July 16, 2018)

"You think too much," my high school boyfriend would tease. He told me this a number of times over our four years of on-again, off-again togetherness. I know it was the result of his own discomfort with being too vulnerable and never meant it to hurt me, but it always stung. I spent some time in my psychology undergrad trying to better understand how/why first loves are so powerful, with potential for lasting effects. Turns out adolescent brain development and hormones raging while trying to navigate a tricky phase of life makes for some pretty sharp and emotionally charged memories. From 17 to 20 years old I was crazy about this boy. I like to think he was pretty crazy about me too, but we were young with no clue of how to hold such big feelings.

He'd come to associate showing emotion with weakness, and was quick to avoid appearances of that. All the while, I'd learned to stay small, please others, keep the important people in my life happy. And this boyfriend was the most important person in my world those days. I remember an ever-present tension in me, wanting badly to get over his walls while never pushing too hard that I got locked out altogether. So, my occasional bids for more open, honest connection were often met with him half-joking, "You think too much" or "Why are we still talking?" And because I had no idea then how to set boundaries or how to ask for what I needed, I rationalized that at least a lot of fun was had during all our not-talking. Interesting how even now I can't read the word "overthink" and not feel some nostalgia for that teenage girl, in love with a boy she was never quite sure felt the same way.

Twenty-plus years out of high school, I've continued to feel the need to either apologize for, explain, or justify my "overthinking." I've ruminated on many unhealthy thoughts or unhelpful memories—still working on that. Yes, I have overthought plenty and have no doubt some witty readers will point out this entire book is case in point of that. Ha! Luckily I've found, or more accurately fostered, a secure enough sense of self that I just don't care. Trying to understand your experiences, patterns of behavior, working to become more self-aware, learning to set and communicate healthy boundaries—that's not overthinking, that's growth, and not something to feel the need to minimize or dismiss. When it came to the 14 inches of hair that had grown with me through the hardest season of my life that I'd just chopped off…Maybe I was overthinking the symbolism, maybe I wasn't, maybe I didn't need it labeled at all, just witnessed.

Microadventures

> Feeling incredibly lucky for beautiful mountains and some seriously tough friends to enjoy them with. We hiked a loop around the cirque yesterday and every step exceeded my expectations. Love the simple calm I feel in these places. Plus, the bugs weren't at all bad, no major injuries, and only one (mostly minor) navigational error. (@megbcampbell July 21, 2018)

Alastair Humphreys, British adventurer and author, popularized the term "microadventure." It's a short, relatively inexpensive, and close to home adventure that should be "fun, exciting, challenging, refreshing and rewarding" (2012). I still can't believe my luck to have found the most amazing girlfriends to plan and go on some pretty epic microadventures with.

Cirque of the Towers, located in the Wind River Mountains of Wyoming, has been a huge hiker and climber destination for decades. I grew up hearing about it from my dad and seeing pictures of the iconic cirque: a semi-circle of jagged granite peaks towering above a high alpine lake and forest. Our plan was to drive up to Big Sandy Trailhead on a Friday afternoon, camp, hike the almost 30-mile loop around the cirque and surrounding area Saturday, camp one more night, and then go home the following Sunday morning.

Things went mostly according to plan, minus the late start and one wrong turn that landed us a short distance below our camp. (I say "below" because I have no idea in what actual direction we headed off course, just know we had to walk uphill to get back.) We were never in any major danger, but finishing an adventure in the dark hours later than planned is never the plan. What's most amazing is that I really can't remember a single person complaining. Sure, we voiced varying opinions and argued over a few route proposals, but never was I anything but overjoyed to be in the company of these beautiful friends. We laughed a lot, we hollered at bears who maybe were or weren't there, we sang as we hiked through huckleberry bushes (trying to scare off said potential bears), we helped each other over Texas Pass, we bushwhacked, we hopped boulders, swatted bugs, crossed streams, and kept putting one foot in front of the other.

I spent a few memorable miles with Madison on this trip. I met Madi years ago upon my moving into the neighborhood where this friend group all lives. We bonded over our love of skiing and running and mountains and have shared numerous microadventures since. I'd been divorced for about four months by this Cirque of the Towers excursion. It was still new. I'd made the Instagram announcement post, cried on a select few bedroom friends' shoulders, thanked many others for their concern and well-wishes, "hearted" many thoughtful text messages—but I hadn't actually spoken about my divorce in detail to hardly anyone. Eventually broaching the topic forced dozens of opportunities to explore and figure out differences between stonewalling, boundaries that protect privacy, genuine vulnerability, and oversharing pretty dang quick. Your story belongs to you and ideally you decide how much you share, when, and with whom.

Still, story sharing is an interesting, far from straight-forward practice. Some people will believe, even insist, they are owed explanations in chapters that have nothing to do with them. Others who deserve explanations never get them, despite their key role in a story. Sometimes trust is broken and people share narratives that were never theirs to tell. It's messy and complicated, to say the least, and others tend to be overly interested in divorce details. Madison never pressed for any, but I felt compelled to share; I had my reasons.

While I say compelled, I was also nervous to the point of stomach butterflies and shaky hands. More holding both: fear and trust, doubt and resolve. My mind raced trying to anticipate her reactions, what would follow, if I was about to make the next 15 miles really awkward, if she would distance herself from me once we returned home. Divorce inevitably costs you a lot, transparency around it may cost you even more. Some people will simply think they know better—know you better, your family better, what would be best for all of you—and then take it personally when you choose differently, behave out of line with values you don't necessarily share, or make mistakes they can't see past.

I had no way of knowing Madi and I wouldn't find ourselves at such an impasse, confiding in her here was a huge leap of faith. And I didn't go on this trip planning to talk about my divorce at all; if anything, I was excited to get away from the many reminders I was, in fact, newly uncoupled. But the clarity with which I'm able to think in these wild spaces, combined with a deep sense that Madi would prove a valuable support, changed my plans.

They won't remember what you said, but they'll remember how you made them feel. Or something along those lines. I've seen variations of this quote most frequently attributed to Maya Angelou on plaques, mugs, cards (you name it!) plenty throughout my teaching career. Educators may be a little burnt out on the quote itself, but I've yet to meet anyone who can deny its truthfulness. I can't recall most of what Madi and I said, but I remember well how I felt. Perhaps it was something about hard truths being spoken and heard in the rugged wilderness our bodies were carrying us through, combined with Madi's simple acceptance of both the ugly and lovely details of my story, of me. I did commit to memory one comforting comment she made, full of hurt and hope and love: "We're adults, Meg. We make choices, live with and learn from consequences, and keep going. That's what we're all doing, and you're doing it remarkably well."

Trusting yourself to know when to trust others with divorce details, or with anything intimate and close to your heart, is tricky; but my vulnerability here let Madi show up in a capacity I didn't realize I needed until I was so relieved to have it. Thank and cherish the sincere friends who show up and hold space, then hopefully pay it forward.

This is Healing

> Brandon sent me this picture from their Pluralsight zoo night and I just love it. I can't decide if I have no words or just far too many to describe the rollercoaster of a transition these past four months have been...There was a point I actually and honestly (and excessively) worried I wouldn't see these beautiful smiles for a long time. Never been so grateful to be so wrong. (@megbcampbell July 22, 2018)

I stared at my phone, tears streaming down my face as I smiled at my three favorite humans smiling back at me. Story had a big blue bat painted across her forehead, wings spread and draped around her eyes. Violet had a feathery pink and red bird wrapping around her left eye, appearing perched on her cheek. On Jude's face, a large black widow spider was painted dangling from a web and crawling along his jaw. I was overwhelmed with more realizations than should try to fit in a single moment. Everything about this picture Brandon had text shook me into some beautiful awareness that they were okay. From the personality-fitting paintings they had each chosen for their faces, to the self-confidence they all smiled at the camera with, to the peaceful energy that just exuded from their bright eyes.

I could write and rewrite, start over and over and over again, keep trying to put into words the immense worry and guilt I felt at how divorce would affect these three. There simply are not words. There's no label for the mental and emotional state I occupied in the months leading up to Brandon moving out, no fitting description for the level or intensity of what I felt. I imagine we all experience something, maybe a number of things, completely unique to us individually— our background, worldview, privilege, current circumstances, values, and hopes all contribute to unique experiences of even relatively common life events, like divorce. Our spoken languages can't possibly encompass such vast and individual experiences of reality. I remember those months on a visceral level, believe they changed me on a cellular level. No way can anyone's brain and body be flooded with that level of stress hormones and not be wired differently upon finally returning to homeostasis.

Or maybe it's difficult to explain in hindsight because time and space and work (always work) have given me tools and perspectives I didn't have then. My memory of the experience gets harder and harder to interpret because now I know so much that I didn't know then; I better understand the fear that I couldn't process then. I have awareness and presence that I couldn't bring to my interactions then. Whatever the reason I struggle to describe this time of my life, this picture woke me up to so much more. It was possible I was wrong about ruining my kids' young lives, possible I could release some fear, let go of some guilt, and redirect all this energy I'd spent worrying endlessly about how divorce would hurt them. Of course, it was more than this picture. I was seeing it every day—my kids were still themselves, still smiling, still pursuing hobbies they loved, still thriving. They were okay.

Sometimes we get accustomed to functioning in chaos, living with heartache, needing to accept difficult truths; but please, please, try to still be open to and look for the good, then let yourself see and relish it when it appears. However fleeting, soak up those realizations and moments because they will help shape the next ones, and this facilitates healing.

Agreements

Just said goodbye to kids. They're going on their first vacation without me. Violet was sobbing, both of us squeezing everything out of that goodbye hug. I remained pretty composed, saw them off before falling completely apart. Feeling so tempted to distract and numb, I'm still convinced long distance running is at least a healthy-ish escape. The beautiful El Vaquero Loco 50K in Wyoming took up a good 24 hours. The company and scenery were lovely, but coming home was rough. I'm having a hard time being alone in my home, but more than that, I'm really struggling with missing the world through my kids' eyes. One of the harshest realities of divorce is that my kids will make and have memories without me. Of course, I want all the happy experiences and memories for them, just selfishly it hurts so impossibly much to miss sharing it. (Journal entry from August 2, 2018)

Whether it was saying bye to my kids for the evening, for a weekend, for a short trip with their dad, I felt such emptiness, sometimes despair, at those goodbyes and my subsequent alone time. Empty from missing them, despair from knowing I chose these circumstances. Difficult feelings, thoughts, and what-ifs would flood my entire being when I was alone. What if one of them gets hurt or feels sad and I'm not there to comfort them? What if the kids want to spend more and more time at their dad's? What if Brandon meets someone new and next year they are on a summer vacation with her? My uncoupling coach Kate was invaluable in helping me challenge this scarcity mentality and redirect my attention, time, and energy in healthier directions.

Kate would often ask me, "Then what?" And I'd play one of my what-if worst-case-scenarios out. She helped me reach the important conclusion that my kids are safe with their dad. *My kids are safe with their dad*, and I could stop my spiraling there. At the time of our divorce, Brandon and I hardly knew each other, certainly didn't know in which direction the other would head, or what choices would be made in the wake of such change and trauma. But I could never deny that my kids were safe with their dad, and how fortunate is that? Until I had any reason to believe otherwise, I needed to let go of what I couldn't control and accept that our family was moving forward on a new path—one of the biggest surrendering practices of my life.

Understanding surrender is much easier to discuss than to do, and after learning some of my history early in our working together, Kate invited me to make a couple key agreements with myself. A big one outlined no sex or alcohol for at least six months after the divorce— take unproductive and detrimental numbing off the table. Kate challenged me to feel it all and throw myself into the work of healing versus defaulting to rather long-established habits of distracting and escaping. I wanted this too and was quick to agree but had no idea just how unaware and out of touch with myself I had grown—maybe had always been. I hadn't been alone, as in alone outside of a romantic relationship, since I was 17 years old. And I'm not sure we can count "alone" time in childhood and adolescence toward understanding and embracing authentic adult identity.

My childhood was certainly privileged and pretty perfect by most standards. Still—and I know this generalizes across generations and genders and cultures, it's not unique to me—I grew up with a great deal of deep-seated fear. I feared failure immensely, feared disappointing my parents, feared the god I believed in until 30 years old, feared mediocrity, feared never being good enough. Not sure how I even defined that back then, I just knew I was always falling short. I was eager to please everyone around me, to gain their affection and approval, combined with any external recognition I could earn (winning ski races, getting good grades, compliments from a boy). These are the things that validated my existence.

My decision-making model became, "How will this decision affect Mom? Will she be pleased or upset, proud or disappointed? What would Mom want me to do?" Later on, "How will this decision affect my friends? What do they think?" And later still, "What does my boyfriend want? I'll do that!" Because by high school, the approval of my current boyfriend had become all-important. It's dangerous entering adolescence without some quality decision-making experience behind you, no solid understanding of cause and effect, without learning to honestly question and intentionally explore, "How will this decision affect me, the quality of my life? What do I really want?"

I have incredible parents who I love dearly; everything they did was out of the deepest love for my sister and me. We were provided every opportunity to pursue our interests and build our best lives. The problem was, I'd been busy building what I believed others thought my best life should look like. At 19 years old, this proved no longer sustainable.

I remember this time now feeling similar in theme to the computer game Dino Run. A simple game with simple graphics; players controlled the little dinosaur character with arrows on the keypad. It was one of the first electronic games my dinosaur-loving Jude ever played. I suspect my memories of him non-stop giggling as he hopped his little Troodon over logs and rocks, only to always be caught by the apocalyptic storm "Doom" closing in behind him—every time exclaiming his disappointment in the cutest little voice, "No, not again!"—is responsible for the fondness I feel toward the analogy now. Like that little Troodon, for a long time I was only aware of a single direction I should be moving, increasingly picking up my pace in an attempt to outrun the fear, dissonance, questions and incongruence (my own personal doom) building behind me.

I had been skiing and racing competitively for about as long as I could remember. I started downhill racing at 6 years old, then switched to Nordic skiing at 12, where I experienced success at the national level as a junior competitor. With this success came expectations and pressure I was ill-prepared to hold. Of course, I didn't connect these dots at the time, but my self-concept and worth were largely rolled up in that success, and I was terrified of slipping.

There was a time I absolutely loved the sport of cross-country skiing and racing. I loved everything about it—exploring mountain trails, pushing my mind and body to their limits. My teammates were some of my best friends. I spent my Thanksgivings in West Yellowstone, Montana, and a week every spring in Bend, Oregon, at training camps. I traveled all over the country for races, ever-marveling at the aurora borealis when racing took me to Alaska, or the peace of Ponderosa State Park when I was fortunate enough to find myself competing in McCall, Idaho (one of my all-time favorite venues). I've worked to integrate these happy memories with the pain and confusion I felt toward the sport when I walked away from it in college. Similar to my feelings toward my past church membership, I am grateful for the sport's influence in shaping who I was, who I am—I try to send this gratitude to any formative path I walked for a time—but leaving it as a young adult triggered a mini-identity crisis that sent me spiraling.

(I only call it "mini" here in comparison to the one that would follow a decade later, but I digress.)

The Dark Ages

> Don't surrender all your joy for an idea you used to have about yourself that isn't true anymore. (Strayed 2015, 6)

Fall of 2001, I was a freshman at Western State College of Gunnison, Colorado (now Western State Colorado University). I'd followed past coaches there, ones I've always adored and admired. (Still do. My first daughter is one of these beloved coaches' namesake.) I hadn't raced well my senior year of high school, so some scholarships I'd been hoping for were no longer available, but I was able to attend Western on a part-athletic, part-academic scholarship.

Where I used to participate in this sport and race with such passion and intensity, I could feel myself burning out. It didn't help that others noticed and expressed their concern—like asking me "what happened" is productive. If I had any clue or ability to turn it around, I would. I was hoping to find some missing piece in Colorado: new team, new scenery, back with my favorite and best coaches. Only in hindsight can I recognize why that wasn't going to happen. My mind and body were trying to continue down a path my heart and core had abandoned. Interesting how long it often takes us to become consciously aware of what we already know on some deeper level. I'd do this same thing— trying to hold on to what I'm no longer meant to—later with my membership in the Mormon church, certain values I grew up with but no longer agreed with, my marriage.

NCAA Division 1 collegiate racing is a massive commitment; you'll be forced to acknowledge if/when you're there for the wrong reasons. The sport was my life. My school and social schedules revolved around my training and racing schedules. I was away from school more days than I was there throughout our competition season, with all the travel it required. Despite this huge time and energy investment, I just couldn't find my drive, couldn't find myself or my joy in this sport any longer.

Plus, I had no space and certainly no tools to hold any more failure. I was no longer finishing on the podium, no longer qualifying for the biggest races, no longer among the best. I didn't know how to reconcile that with who I believed I was supposed to be, and I couldn't fix this for all those I was disappointing. I was done, but exiting at my young age and under the circumstances, I wasn't due a peaceful retirement.

After getting back from a week of racing in Anchorage the spring of my freshman year, I rather impulsively reached out to my longtime, childhood friend who was living in Logan, Utah, and studying at Utah State University. I told her I was transferring to USU next year and asked if I could live with her. She said of course, and the next steps transpired fast. I applied to USU that evening, feeling rushed to get certain plans in place before others would inevitably try to talk me out of them.

I can't recall exactly when I told my parents. I just remember dreading it, and sure enough, it wasn't pretty. Being a parent myself now, I can better imagine the hurt and disappointment this decision caused. My parents had invested in these goals and dreams for 15 years; to have no say when I chose to drop them must have been incredibly frustrating. Not to mention college tuition was no longer covered; simply from a practical standpoint, my decision to walk away from scholarships was hard to understand, much less support.

It was after a particularly difficult phone call with my mom that I hung up and tasted my first sip of alcohol. I'd had opportunities to drink before, but it'd been relatively easy to avoid for a number of reasons: fear of addiction (I'd been warned it "ran in the family" and understood it wouldn't be tolerated growing up), fear of God (it was against the "Word of Wisdom" that my then-church taught), fear of it hurting my overall fitness; plus, our team had agreed to a dry season. But the season was over, my ski racing career was over, and my give-a-damn completely broke.

Wish I could have embraced Cheryl Strayed's wisdom then—wisdom not yet recorded at the time—but wish I could have believed it was okay to change goals, plans, paths altogether upon realizing a current one is void of the joy once experienced on it. Ideas we have about ourselves—who we are, who we want to be—of course some are bound to change. This was one of many intersections where I struggled to embrace necessary change. I was embarrassed, confused, and horribly unprepared to lose this primary identity of "competitive athlete." I grew restless without a team, without a coach telling me how much to eat, sleep, and train, with extra time I had no idea how to fill. This would have been the perfect chapter in my young life to engage in more exploring, soul-searching, and core-listening; instead, I practiced numbing, pretending, escaping straight into my dark ages.

Incongruence

> Brave is matching your insides and outsides…Actions are not inherently brave—the honoring of the inner compass instead of the outer expectation is the braveness. (Doyle 2021)

Like so many of us, I've been accustomed to major incongruence between my insides and outsides, often hustling to meet the latest outside demands. With my decision to quit competing, I'd never fallen so short of those external expectations, and it felt awful. And this is one reason alcohol is so dangerous—it gives you a false sense of congruence when true congruence would require work you're either not aware of or not ready and willing to do yet. It feels like your insides and outsides match; it makes you feel less awful, if only for a brief period.

It took some time to start processing what leaving the sport meant for me. Initially, I was so overwhelmed with attempting to dull the pain of disappointing my parents, insisting to my coach that I wasn't changing my mind, trying to rationalize my decision to teammates. (I'd find myself in similar situations and conversations later in life explaining/defending my decision to leave a church, my decision to get divorced—still hard to own hard choices, even when they're the right ones.) When I was sober, I felt alone, confused, scared of what was next because I couldn't picture myself or my daily life without the sport. It felt almost reckless to be ignoring so many of my life's prescribed "shoulds"—you should keep ski racing, you should keep your scholarships, you should appreciate this opportunity, you should take advantage of getting to travel, you should enjoy time being made for you to maintain the best shape of your life, you should be grateful!

While drinking helped me escape some of these reminders most nights, I'd wake up in major shame spirals because drinking alcohol was itself counter to my religious values and upbringing. So now, not only had I walked away from ski racing, I'd fallen out of good standing in my church. I was running out of viable identity options! The more incongruence I felt, the more I'd drink to feel a fake sense of alignment, and before long I was sneaking vodka in Nalgene water bottles to the library with me to study. We know it's a vicious cycle.

The Invitation

It doesn't interest me
what you do for a living.
I want to know
what you ache for
and if you dare to dream
of meeting your heart's longing.

It doesn't interest me
how old you are.
I want to know
if you will risk
looking like a fool
for love
for your dream
for the adventure of being alive.

It doesn't interest me
what planets are
squaring your moon...
I want to know
if you have touched
the center of your own sorrow,
if you have been opened

by life's betrayals
or have become shriveled and closed
from fear of further pain.

I want to know
if you can sit with pain,
mine or your own,
without moving to hide it
or fade it
or fix it.

I want to know
if you can be with joy
mine or your own,
if you can dance with wildness
and let the ecstasy fill you
to the tips of your fingers and toes
without cautioning us
to be careful
to be realistic
to remember the limitations
of being human.

It doesn't interest me
if the story you are telling me
is true.
I want to know if you can
disappoint another
to be true to yourself.
If you can bear
the accusation of betrayal
and not betray your own soul.
If you can be faithless
and therefore trustworthy.
I want to know if you can see Beauty
even when it is not pretty
every day.
And if you can source your own life
from its presence.

I want to know
if you can live with failure,
yours and mine,
and still stand at the edge of the lake
and shout to the silver of the full moon,
"Yes."

It doesn't interest me
to know where you live
or how much money you have.
I want to know if you can get up
after the night of grief and despair
weary and bruised to the bone
and do what needs to be done
to feed the children.

It doesn't interest me
who you know
or how you came to be here.
I want to know if you will stand
in the center of the fire
with me
and not shrink back.
It doesn't interest me
where or what or with whom
you have studied.
I want to know
what sustains you
from the inside
when all else falls away.

I want to know
if you can be alone
with yourself
and if you truly like
the company you keep
in the empty moments.
(Oriah 1999)

That was a lot of backstory to explain Kate's invitation to me: to work *through* the terrifying life transition of divorce, instead of around it by numbing the hurt or running from the unknown. Upon a friend first sharing this poem, I realized how deeply I ached to meet and know me, to access some inner compass. I couldn't say I liked the company I kept when alone. I would get physically restless and claustrophobic, couldn't be alone and content at the same time; it was uncomfortable at best, but usually rather unbearable, making alcohol all the more tempting.

Diego Perez articulates this discomfort well. "Hard truth: Your relationship with silence will reflect how at home you feel within your own mind and body. If you need to constantly get away from yourself, there is unprocessed pain within you that needs attention and care" (2023). Divorce, combined with Kate's invitation at 34 years old to feel it all, to stop resisting and work through it, would force me to finally address unprocessed pain, to finally find and return to myself.

Not only did divorce highlight my dislike of being alone, but also how much I craved external validation. It was an intense craving, born of various unmet needs and broken places. While divorce won't show everyone the same things, it will expose damaged pieces and open gaping holes that marriage and a partner and all that previous structure had served to cover up, but never actually heal.

One weekend night shortly after my divorce, I was out to dinner with a few good girlfriends. I laughed out loud at the idea of ever dating again when the subject came up. I explained I was way more stressed about things like how I was going to continue to afford my house, support my kids' increasingly expensive hobbies, and the zero retirement dollars I had saved. I had recently made the mistake of Googling suggestions of how much one "should" have saved by my age—*ummm, uh-oh!* Some days this weighed on me heavily, other days I could dismiss it as a problem for future me; but it was certainly more pressing than the idea of dating again.

Liza (remember my wise therapist friend) couldn't help but interject here. "Back up, back up, back way up. Let's table the dating talk, and we are absolutely not talking about retirement plans, or lack thereof right now. You are Swiss cheese, my friend." She is referencing all of me with those full-palm, hand circles in my direction. "Literally holes everywhere."

I was Swiss cheese. The holes were huge and many, and they freaking hurt.

Chances are, if you're reading this, you may feel like Swiss cheese too. Your own unique slice, but I bet you know the holes. They're whatever you're desperate to numb and escape. And the desperation to escape is powerful, animalistic, and urgent. Your brain honestly thinks you are in real danger and quite possibly going to die from how scary and painful these exposed holes are, triggering stress response after stress response. *You are not going to die.* Read this to yourself aloud, remind yourself while engaging in nervous system regulation practices: *You are safe. You will survive this.* Then make a plan for how you will survive the next moment, how you'll resist the urge to escape, how you'll face the hard, how you'll be kind to yourself when you slip up. It'll take time, awareness, gracious intention and work, but those holes will start to heal. Embrace Liza's permission to pursue and allow that healing over feeling anxious to check other boxes or force other paths.

Swiss Cheese and Sidewalk Holes

Autobiography in Five Short Chapters

I. I walk down the street. There is a deep hole in the sidewalk. I fall in. I am lost. I am helpless. It isn't my fault. It takes forever to find a way out.

II. I walk down the same street. There is a deep hole in the sidewalk. I still don't see it. I fall in again. I can't believe I am in the same place. It isn't my fault. It still takes a long time to get out.

III. I walk down the same street. There is a deep hole in the sidewalk. I see it there, I still fall in. It's a habit. It's my fault. I know where I am. I get out immediately.

IV. I walk down the same street. There is a deep hole in the sidewalk. I walk around it.

V. I walk down a different street. (Nelson 2012)

Kate shared this piece with me one visit in 2018 when I was feeling particularly discouraged at what felt like slow progress. It became a favorite reminder I read often through that Swiss cheese phase. Themes of acceptance and surrender were (still are) forever recurring, and the need for self-compassion ever present.

It'll be tempting to blame and demean yourself for the exposed Swiss cheese holes, for the hole in your sidewalk you're continually falling in—but be gentle. Treat yourself the way you would a dear friend attempting to do the work of growing more self-aware. Understand that taking new ownership resulting from finally acknowledging and addressing problematic habits and behaviors is scary and exhausting. Trying to do better upon knowing better is something to support and celebrate, both in others and ourselves.

The Uintas

> Of the many places we've explored in these mountains, I think we found a new favorite. Long, Duck, and Island Lakes area…in love! Less in love with the funk I've been in since returning from such a special weekend with Brandon and kids in the Uintas. It was beautiful and pretty perfect, maybe I'm still trying to make sense of it. Seeing our kids overjoyed to be all together as a family is bittersweet—I'm grateful we can make it happen, I feel guilty it's not under the circumstances I assume they'd rather. Maybe it will always feel a little sad that their parents couldn't love each other better? (@runwriteheal August 12, 2018)

We know our bodies are capable of holding on to emotional energy. We know sometimes it gets trapped. Eckhart Tolle teaches about pain bodies, Bessel van der Kolk has outlined how *The Body Keeps the Score* (2014), Carl Jung taught us that what we resist persists, and Brené

Brown has emphasized that owning our story is what ultimately allows us to write daring endings. I've appreciated these resources in trying to explore and work on my dark corners. But the Uinta mountain range is the opposite, a truly bright spot. These mountains live in me—the associations, the memories, the feelings elicited when I revisit those memories. I can sense these mountains in my cells, they're familiar at my core, they feel like home.

The Uinta Mountains are located primarily in northeastern Utah, running some into southern Wyoming. It's the highest mountain range running east to west in the lower 48 states and contains the highest point in Utah, Kings Peak, reaching an elevation of 13,528 feet. The Uintas consist largely of quartzite, slate, and shale rock, allowing the range to hold a lot of water. There are thousands of lakes and ponds, and hundreds of miles of streams. I've spent countless hours and steps exploring these special mountains.

As a young girl, I remember backpacking trips to a few family-favorite destinations: Divide, Ibantik, Cuberant, and Amethyst Lakes. I've since returned with my own kids to these places. Something about my youthful memories of these spaces and getting to witness my kids meet and explore them is so special, wondering if they'll also grow up to feel at home here.

My first time up Kings Peak was with my junior cross-country ski team in 1997. I recall my ramen noodles our first night looked covered in thick pepper; I was disgusted to realize just how impossible it'd be to separate my noodles from all the mosquitoes I'd boiled with them. My coaches (those near and dear to me ones I'd later follow to Colorado) joked that it was a good source of protein. I remember the intense afternoon thunderstorms that hurt my ears and shook the ground. I can still visualize the helicopter landing below Gunsight Pass to extract the body of a man who'd been struck by lightning on the exposed ridge leading up to the peak.

It was wild for my 14-year-old brain to process that, while I was huddled well below timberline waiting out the most powerful storm I'd ever witnessed, another hiker was struck and killed just a matter of miles and a few hundred vertical feet from me. I felt sick trying to imagine the panic he must have felt upon realizing he was too high, too exposed, that it may be too late. I guessed at various easy-to-make mistakes, perhaps believing he had enough time, could beat the storm, that the summit's *right there*. I could majorly empathize with summit-fever, so the thought of that possibility shook me up pretty good. Or maybe he'd rolled an ankle, ran out of water, or his muscles were cramping as a result of the thinner air at that elevation. For whatever reason, he couldn't descend as quickly as planned and needed. How terrifying that must have been.

We summited as a team the next day. The experience was incredible and sobering. As we made our way up the talus field toward the top, I found myself thinking often of this stranger whose life had ended here the day before, checking the time every so often and scanning all directions for signs of an imminent storm. We all were, and that group awareness probably contributed to my coach's insistence we hustle back down. We spent a whole two minutes atop Utah's highest peak taking in the amazing 360-degree view, barely enough time to catch our breath and snap a few pictures before booking it back below timberline and to the safety of our sheltered camp, where we piled into a tent and played card games through the afternoon storms.

I vaguely remember packing up the next morning; my shoulders ached and a few blisters were bothering me now that I had my heavy pack on. It was a long slog back to the trailhead, then I was both relieved and a little bummed to see our team van waiting in the parking lot. It'd been an intense three days spent laughing, worrying, playing, consoling one another, working together, pushing limits, and growing closer. I wasn't ready for it to end. I'm not sure how to name that feeling, but it's familiar to the human experience—a little sad something is ending, mixed with an understanding such things inevitably do, a little wanting to believe you'll experience it again. We made a pact to repeat this adventure in 10 years, and the thought of a reunion trip made me happy.

But that tenth summer came and went with no return to Kings Peak, no mention of it. I didn't totally forget but also didn't entertain the possibility of doing anything to make it happen. We'd all scattered into our adult worlds, and I chuckled at how naive we were to think we'd return together a decade later.

Now, closer to 20 years after that pact was made, I'm not eye-rolling or laughing at such teenage agreements, I instead find them rather charming. More often than not, such youthful promises aren't or can't be honored come adulthood. But I love that we don't know that, nor do we think to question it at the time. The notion of demanding jobs, living far away from one another, marriage, divorce, kids of our own, and other responsibilities that would prevent a dozen of us from coming together and pulling off this kind of trip in the Uinta backcountry was just too foreign. How amazing to be granted a handful of blissfully ignorant, lighthearted adolescent years.

Story of Us

It's comparable to the bliss we experience in the early years of romantic relationships. Things like frustration with and resentment toward our partner, habits we once found endearing growing painfully obnoxious, somehow feeling lonely in the presence of our person—there was a time those possibilities were inconceivable too.

Dr. Gottman (1994) has researched and written about the Story of Us. He explains that how couples recall and tell the start of their relationship story says a lot about the current state of their relationship and how likely it is to survive the hardships that inevitably surface in all partnerships. Some couples will recount their stories rather positively, highlighting the good and the effort to grow their relationship, remembering their partner and still retrieving those early memories through a rose-colored lens. Other couples will tell their Story of Us negatively; even once-objectively happy memories have been tainted by toxic interactions and contempt. We're sure our partner has always been the problem, we plant red flags in places they never initially occupied, we've convinced ourselves the relationship has been rough and wrong from the start.

Toward the end of my marriage, while Brandon and I were grateful that our relationship resulted in our kids, our Story of Us was otherwise pretty pessimistic. We even worked with a Gottman therapist with whom we both formally completed the Story of Us exercise. At the time, both Brandon and I recalled a rather bleak beginning, struggling to recount many happy details about our relationship's origin or even how/why we fell for each other in the first place. I'm happy to say that time, space, and work (always work!) have served to clear some of that brain fog.

How incredible that a conscious uncoupling managed to rewrite my Story of Us; that I can now remember beautiful and joyful memories of my relationship with Brandon, memories that had all but completely drowned under the weight of a marriage that was no longer working but we were trying to force.

Divorce gifted both old and new happy memories. I couldn't believe I was back in my favorite mountains with my beloved kids and former husband on our first backpacking trip since the divorce. *Are we crazy? Who does this?!* I wondered. The months before and through the whole divorce process, I had no idea what the future held. I often assumed the worst, some nights convincing myself Brandon would be dating a gorgeous, brilliant 21-year-old aerospace engineer (his profession at the time of our split) the minute our divorce was final. We even added an agreement into our final papers that our kids wouldn't meet a new partner until a year minimum after the divorce. (There was no directive of what Brandon and I could or couldn't do individually, just that our personal, romantic lives wouldn't intersect with the kids' that first year.) However immature that might sound, I've come to believe this was a genius request. To guarantee our kids a year to adjust to their new normal before throwing Mom or Dad's new boyfriend/girlfriend into the mix seems reasonable enough; but since it was also made from a place of scarcity and total fear of the unknown…hard to insist it's sound advice.

If it had anything to do with providing this chance to backpack into the Uintas together again as a family, I don't care about the underlying motivation, it was worth it. I had been devastated at the thought of family adventures looking different, it was one of those eventualities I was most broken over when deciding to divorce. Not that I wouldn't feel comfortable still taking the kids on various excursions myself; we could continue to do plenty of hiking, skiing, and exploring. But I knew there'd be other adventures I wouldn't feel comfortable or responsible attempting without Brandon, or him without me. Backpacking, canyoneering, rock climbing, scaling big peaks—any large undertaking requiring things like rope work, route finding, or problem-solving in the moment, with the potential for big consequences—deserves both parents. I was acutely aware of the need to balance my desire to still do all of these things with young kids, with how potentially risky it might be to attempt solo. I couldn't put them in unnecessary danger made necessary by their parents' decision to divorce.

Precedents

Despite there being a time I would have sworn up and down that Brandon and I would never again collaborate on family adventures, I suppose this first Uinta trip came about as a result of us both ultimately wanting our family to continue to share these experiences, even if it meant major awkwardness for us. We decided to head somewhere new, an area I'd never before explored in child- or adulthood. It seemed fitting to walk into the unknown—no past associations, only the potential for new memories as a newly reorganized family. I was pretty discouraged at first when some stomach bug or food poisoning (or maybe just the physical result of accumulated stress and worry) hit me not even a mile in. Brandon and I were in a fragile place. I wanted to be present and invest my energy in helping this trip go smoothly, not sick and throwing up, figuring out how to heave with a heavy pack on and not tip over (since backpacking with kids is anything but light and minimal).

Brandon read me well, asked what I needed, took some items from my pack and strapped them to his, but he didn't argue when I insisted I wanted to keep going and could sense this would pass. Sure enough, and thankfully, it did. By the time we reached our destination and found the loveliest spot to camp along the outskirts of Long Lake, I was feeling much better. Brandon slept in a hammock, the kids and I in the tent. Between all my puking on the hike in and our sleeping arrangements looking different than past trips, the first night felt uncomfortable; but we were together in the Uintas, and I could tolerate a lot of discomfort for that.

After breakfast the next morning, we hiked to Duck Lake, then onto Island Lake a little farther, where we found a quiet and picturesque lunch spot. I sat down on the sunny slab of rock that inclined slightly into the water below, looking at the peaks above me, my people around me—so much to absorb. These mountains…I love these mountains. And my sweet kids who I love more than anything. There I sat for some time—still and surrounded by love.

To my left, our chocolate lab Molly can't contain her excitement as Violet throws a stick into the water for her to retrieve. Ahead of me, Jude is stripping down to his underwear to brave the freezing water, asking who dares him to put his head under (we all do). To my left, Story is flossing—the dance, not the dental hygiene kind—pleased with finally getting the alternating hip-arm swing rhythm down. And there's Brandon; he'd continued down to about knee-deep in the lake below me, seemingly also lost in thought.

Five years later I asked him what he remembered about the trip. "I remember trying to convince myself that what mattered most hadn't really changed. Our legal status was different, and we were living in different homes, but our relationships with the kids were still central and strong, and you and I could only stand to get better from there.

We were all physically healthy, our lives overall remained really great if we could focus on the good. Being out in the mountains away from the heaviness we were feeling at home made it easier to embrace that perspective and even appreciate our overall circumstances."

That wisdom right there is gold. When life feels heavy and dark, try to zoom out and look for the good. Usually, it's our compulsive thoughts about a hard situation that make the situation so hard, certainly more difficult than it objectively is. The Uintas provided this broader perspective for both Brandon and me. I am forever grateful we managed to establish a precedent early on of prioritizing our family. It's an ongoing practice of humility and strength, presence and foresight, surrender and work.

The Universe (Shoving)

> Ten years ago, I was a semester away from finishing my master of education degree when I learned I was pregnant with Jude. I put school on hold and began teaching kindergarten full time because we needed the insurance. I can't imagine doing a thing different now. I'm glad we started a family and have the kids that we do...Jude, Vi and Story are my all-time favorite humans, the most beautiful things I've ever been a part of. It's all worked out as it should, and I'm excited now to be finally returning to finish that degree. It's crazy to be back on the Logan campus today. I feel old! (@megbcampbell August 22, 2018)

My dear bedroom friend Shera once sent me an image of a giant hand, representing the Universe, literally pushing a human figure (labeled You) off a cliff. Below the cliff's edge was another giant hand, labeled Also The Universe, there to catch the falling figure (You). This visual comes to mind when I think back on this time, particularly the shoving part.

It was the best and worst time to return to graduate school. I wonder if perhaps I threw myself into way more than I should have thought reasonable at the time. I was navigating this major life change that resulted from divorce, trying to not only keep up with my kids' schedules, but show up for them in a capacity and with the presence I both valued and felt I'd missed so much over the past few years. (Not that I physically missed much. I was physically there for just about everything, but often distracted, lost in my own mess of sadness, confusion, and mistakes.)

I was also working full-time, training for a 100-mile trail race, and now about to start graduate school. I look back on these years and struggle to fathom what I was thinking or how we managed it. I'm sure there was a less-conscious component of staying busy enough to stay ahead of the hurt. I've also just barely skimmed the surface of better understanding goal setting as a trauma response...hmmm. Maybe not ideal, but it's where I found myself.

It was the spring of 2018, shortly after my divorce was final, when I received a notification from Utah State University that it'd been nearly 10 years since I'd first applied to and started graduate school. The communication explained that if I didn't enroll the following semester, my graduate application and acceptance would expire. It was now or never. As easy as it would have been to claim I'd return eventually, to rationalize putting it off a few more years, I also knew how unlikely it was I'd ever take the GRE again, could guess I wouldn't make the time to write new application essays or ask for new letters of recommendation, wouldn't get around to whatever other admissions requirements I'd long since forgotten. I knew better than to try and convince myself I'd do this "later."

Plus, the thought of going back to school was both exhilarating and oddly comforting. I've always been good at school. At a time I was feeling like a lousy wife and had just failed at marriage, I trusted my identity as a competent student. The prospect of returning to an arena where I felt a strong sense of self-efficacy was a welcome adventure; it felt good to pursue and invest in a goal that was mine, as I'd always wanted to finish my MEd.

Occasionally, when I'd feel major mom guilt over the bad timing of my return to school or when I'd feel super discouraged sitting down to hours of homework after putting the kids to bed, I'd remind myself that time will pass regardless, and I just needed to determine what had to be done next. Moving next right thing to next right thing, trusting this was not only a good thing for me, but also a good thing for my kids to see me do for me. Stepping out of my comfort zone to return to the kind of work I hadn't done in a decade—reading, studying, taking exams, writing papers, completing projects—all of which I really didn't have time for yet somehow made the time. My brain literally hurt at first, partly from the schoolwork and learning, partly from trying to keep up with my life and all I'd chosen to be accountable for through this season, leaning into the familiar-yet-brand-newness of it all, trying to trust the universe both shoves and catches.

Beautiful Souls

I've gone to write something about this at least a dozen times over the past few months, but I get all emotional and can't find the right words to express how incredibly in awe I am of the many beautiful souls I get to call friends.

Back in April, when I turned down offers to go out and celebrate my birthday (I was being a little, maybe a lot antisocial), these friends came in and deep cleaned my house, leaving the most thoughtful gifts, cards and a birthday caricature poster with words of encouragement. Just recently, while I was in California, they re-did my bedroom and I am absolutely obsessed with it. Such an enormous labor of love.

The countless acts of kindness…Whether it's an anonymous grocery gift card left in my mailbox, helping watch my kids, listening to me on a long run, going on an adventure, singing Indigo Girls at the top of our lungs…I could go on and on and on.

They show up for me and remind me how to show up too. They see and love me through the times I've felt more lost than ever. They are bright, kind, and real. They've always been there, holding space with lots of love and acceptance…These experiences have been among the most humbling of my life.

Daily I see this poster hanging in my closet. Every day I just love love love my room—such beautiful and powerful reminders of their faith in me. I don't know how I got so lucky.

I hope you all know who you are. You make me want to do and be better, to choose love every day, every time. Thank you. (@megbcampbell August 28, 2018)

I've mentioned I have truly remarkable friends. I realize how fortunate I am for this support system. I also believe I've been drawn to these authentic women as I've worked to live more honestly and with a more abundant mindset myself. I wrote the above post in 2018. In 2023, the caricature Shera drew of me running happy, wild, and free remains hanging in my closet, and I remain in awe of the love and kindness these friends continually gift me, including through the seasons I've been unable to adequately reciprocate.

I'm sharing this here as a hopeful reminder to look for love and goodwill. Look for who is trying to show you these things, and look for who is trying to just figure out how to show you these things. I've been pleasantly surprised by friends thanking me for communicating how I'd like them to act through my divorce. Of course, the immediate family is most impacted by one couple's divorce, but it's still confusing for everyone it reaches, near and far—friends, your kids' friends, extended family, neighbors, your kids' teachers, coaches, school personnel—they would probably welcome some guidance. Anywhere you can exert influence to shape a healthy narrative of your uncoupling, do it!

For Brandon and me, obvious examples of this include that "divorce announcement" we shared on social media and the various posts I've addressed our co-parenting relationship in since. We've explicitly asked for grace and compassion from everyone for all of us—no sides, no blaming, only love. Other times I've tried to redirect conversations, refusing to participate in bad-mouthing Brandon or gossiping about our situation. And this isn't to say there weren't times I badly wanted to, but I did my best to save my venting, my meltdowns, my unloading for Kate, and occasionally a bedroom friend that I trusted was a total vault. Perhaps this is partly why I was so antisocial for a good five months, and that was okay.

I couldn't completely trust myself because there were times my best efforts to save it for appropriate sharing spaces weren't good enough, and I regretted slipping up and sharing either more than I should have or totally inaccurate details about our situation with those who didn't need to hear it. I now try to keep in mind that my story of the divorce and understanding of reasons behind it are ever-changing and evolving. Much of what I thought I *needed* others to hear and understand five years ago now seems irrelevant or completely absurd.

Instagram just happened to work for me as a helpful tool to control my divorce narrative. I figured it'd reach the family and friends I needed it to, especially given the small community we live in, where my kids go to school, where I teach kindergarten, where I guessed members of my previous faith would attribute the divorce to us leaving the church; I wanted a say. I understood people would talk, speculate, and that rumors would circulate; I'd never have the last word, but I was stubborn about having the first, then updating and clarifying over the years. (Important disclaimer: Stay far, far away from social media if you aren't in a place to post civilly and responsibly about your divorce. You can be sad, hurt, vulnerable, and real; but the second you start bitching about your former partner or divorce details—I don't care how valid you feel your points are—unloading on social media is immature, usually impulsive, and makes you look like the asshat. Try to align and lead with love!)

Besides, despite there being various options and platforms for communicating hopes and expectations for others' conduct with regard to your divorce, really, it's your own behavior that will do the most influencing and updating. One small practice I continue today in conversation with others is using labels like "former husband," "co-parent," "Jude/Violet/Story's dad" over the label of "ex" when referring to Brandon. It used to make me especially uncomfortable when someone would refer to him as my ex in front of or within earshot of our kids. Their dad will never be x-ed out of their mom's life, and the thought of them thinking their parents could ever view the other like that made me sad. At first, I never said anything as Brandon is, by definition, an ex-husband to me. It took some time for me to get brave and confident enough to challenge this commonplace label. It's easier now, probably because it's become more accurate to refer to him as a good friend, great dad and/or ideal co-parent anyway.

It's likely easy to say you want friends to not pick sides, to support both of you, to love your unconventional family really big— sounds amazing and certainly the ideal—but it takes so much grace to actually let them, your people, practice it. My friends coordinated all the incredible service I mentioned above with Brandon so they could surprise me. He knew my schedule best because it was the kids' schedule, he knew I was on a morning-long field trip with Story and out of the house for the birthday deep-clean, he was even dog-sitting for me while the kids and I were visiting grandparents in San Diego during that bedroom remodel week. I still cannot believe Brandon was in a place to collaborate in these capacities for me. Like me, he'd only been divorced a matter of months and was living with similar pain. Everything was different and new and scary for him too; yet he was so kind and mature in his treatment of me.

It would have been easy for him to not want any part of these remodel plans. What possible motivation could he have for helping friends completely redo the bedroom he and I shared for the past 10 years in that home? It brings me to tears that he was willing to help my friends show me love. Instead of choosing to write it off as not his problem—because it absolutely was not his problem that I was having a hard time healing in that bedroom—he chose compassion. He helped my dear friends see a need and fill it, without questioning if I was deserving of that kind of investment and attention from them or not.

Hurting a Parent of Your Kids Hurts Your Kids

Your family is a microculture. The unique fingerprint of you and your spouse. The weaving of bones. Divorce, in turn, is the dissolution of such. The severing of a limb to save the tree. A metamorphosis that is characterized more by coming undone than by becoming. For the first time, you and your partner will have to venture into something together that is, by definition, designed to be done alone. You will go through divorce alone, together.

In my work as a couple's therapist, if a couple with children decides to divorce, I caution them that this is a time when they must be careful. I remind them that most likely, their bodies have come to recognize the other as the enemy and that given this, their heart rates will increase to over 100 beats per minute whenever they are in close proximity to the other. For many, this physiological response to threat will occur even at the mere thought of the other.

And while these biological alarms may very well prepare you for war, they also come at a cost. Diffuse physiological arousal (DPA) is the amalgam of bodily stress responses. In addition to an accelerated heart rate, DPA is characterized by an increase in stress hormones. The result is an inability to think, communicate, or hear clearly.

Not surprisingly, divorce is a time when you will struggle with periods of psychological, physiological, and emotional impairment. All of this occurring while you are simultaneously called on to make critical decisions, single-parent, generate income, sell or relocate your home, and navigate the grief and loss of dreams. Your life is coming undone faster than you can rebuild it, and the seeds of regeneration have yet to sprout their tendrils.

According to Dr. John Gottman, author of *Raising an Emotionally Intelligent Child*, if you want to know whether a kid is navigating parental crisis at home, there's a litmus test. It turns out that children exposed to "great marital hostility" have markedly higher levels of stress hormones than children of parents with stable marriages.

Remember this when you're seething in anger at your ex-to-be, and it threatens to overtake you. Your kid will excrete toxins of distress that their body cannot possibly metabolize. By a familial nervous system, you are all still interconnected on a subterranean level, and their body is screaming "stop," even if they never utter a word to you. (Lusignan 2019)

I try to engage in perspective taking and have immense empathy for people deeply hurting through the end of a marriage, but I struggle to understand divorcing couples who spend excessive time, energy, and money aiming to ensure their former partner suffers miserably. I understand the need to feed an ego can be powerful, especially while trying to protect ourselves through the loss of a core attachment. It's normal and natural that we feel inclined to fight; but stop, please stop. Especially when kids are involved. Hurting a parent of your kids hurts your kids, the end.

Perhaps the kindest thing you can manage is wanting to want to stop, but your wisest self is being constantly flooded with pain and rage, and you can't seem to end a vicious cycle of damaging and destructive behavior. This is another crossroads where reaching out and obtaining professional help is crucial. Behavior is the result of so much past conditioning, possibly unprocessed trauma, plenty of childhood and attachment stuff, neural wiring and patterns that are really difficult to just turn around on your own. A coach or therapist is invaluable to this work.

Anything you think you gain by intentionally hurting your former partner is a dangerous and ugly illusion. Please don't entertain it.

Collective Healing

I didn't record this anywhere until now, so I can only guess at the time frame. It was after the bedroom remodel, but within a year, maybe a year and a half of my divorce.

Keep in mind, Brandon and I spent a good deal of time with our closest couple friends while married. A number of us had even left the LDS church within a few years of each other. May sound ridiculous, but a faith crisis then exodus from the church in a rural Utah community will serve to bond you. These were our people. After our divorce, and in attempts to honor our joint request that they not feel any need to pick sides or exclude either one of us, they continued putting us both on group texts and invites, everything ranging from planning weekend hangouts to holiday parties.

For months neither Brandon nor I went to these. I had no desire to face the discomfort I guessed would be waiting for me at those get-togethers; I couldn't even visualize myself getting to the front door alone, much less entering and socializing. We both told each other, "You can go...You could totally go...You should go..." Then, get this, one of those times Brandon finally went, and I lost my mind.

My reaction shocked me. I missed that split second to redirect, anger overcame me, and big emotions completely hijacked my upstairs brain. Everything about my response was completely unreasonable. But why, why was I so upset? Like vision-blurring-can't-think-straight pissed about this? Did I think he'd never go, never re-engage one day? Was I simply upset he beat me to it? My heart was pounding in my throat, rage coursing through my body; I was furious, sweaty, and shaky, and before I could stop myself, I started moving this intense energy through awful texts to Brandon: *How could you? Those are my friends. That's so hurtful you would go while I'm here getting the kids tucked in night after night. You don't think I'd like to go out? How are you so insensitive?!* Super sucks to admit, but on I raged.

This wasn't a completely brand-new experience, being overcome with feelings of animosity and anger. It was triggered more frequently in me through the middle of our divorce but surprised me all these months later. I went to bed fuming mad that night, then awoke the next morning, calm and embarrassed. It took another couple of months to become more aware of how hypocritical I'd been. Truly wanting our friends to continue loving and showing up for Brandon and me means not only asking them to, but meeting them in the middle again. I needed to let go enough to give both Brandon and myself permission to move toward them in new ways.

It may be difficult to see your former partner healing. Even if/when it is genuinely what you want, it'll understandably hurt to ever feel left behind. It will sting to see a past love be okay, even healthier, without you. That scarcity mentality is natural and tempting to embrace at this point—wanting to "win" the breakup, move on first, seem better off and more okay than you really are. Remind yourself this is not a race; another's progress and growth takes nothing away from your own. We are each responsible for our individual healing and happiness. You should have never been the source of that for another anyway, so don't take it personally when they pursue it outside of your relationship. This is a good thing, even when it doesn't feel good.

Practice lots of self-care and self-compassion, remember you are accountable for yourself, your journey—if you can manage to be honestly happy for others' healing while working on your own, you are part of the solution and are making this world better! Brandon understood and embraced this abundant perspective earlier than I did: any and everyone's healing is good for humanity. Our world needs more souls who value our collective healing, my most sincere thanks!

Gestures of Goodwill

> I went to Brandon's youngest brother's wedding last weekend. Hands down one of the hardest things I've done post-divorce. Seeing his family, watching him and the kids go take pictures without me, seeing my beloved family that isn't the same family anymore. And seriously, just look at those bright, beautiful kids. Still don't believe this will ever feel completely okay. (@runwriteheal September 18, 2018)

Man, this was rough. Telling our kids about the divorce was the hardest thing, but I'm calling this a close second. I was positive I wouldn't go to this wedding, borderline offended even that anyone would think it reasonable for me to attend. I'd been invited, and the kids of course wanted me to go. While I'd known this brother of Brandon's since he was 5 years old, I had no relationship of really any substance with him in adulthood. I also had very little interest in seeing Brandon's extended family under these new circumstances; I didn't want to field questions about our divorce or participate in uncomfortable conversations all evening.

I brought all of this up in one of my visits with my uncoupling coach Kate, totally thinking she'd respond with something like, *Agreed, that's asking way too much of you...No way you should feel obligated to go... They aren't your in-laws anymore, no need to rationalize or explain your absence.* Instead, she invited me to explore the information in front of me:

- You've been extended an invitation.
- You have no actual schedule conflicts.
- Brandon, his family, and most importantly your kids have all expressed hope that you'll attend.

She pointed out that's a lot of goodwill that's been extended to me, and then we dove into my reasons for not wanting to respond in kind.

"It'll be so awkward. It's too soon. I don't want to see them yet, and at a wedding no less, a celebration of the very thing we just failed at...I won't know how to act, I don't want to fake being more okay than I am all night...Plus, marriage is stupid, why do we still celebrate such a silly practice? Divorced people just don't go to ex-in-laws' weddings!" I went on and on; I had reasons to skip it coming out my ears.

Kate listened patiently and acknowledged this was a difficult decision. She then referenced something we'd spoken about often— how a successful conscious uncoupling is made up of many gestures of goodwill, both big and small. These thoughtful gestures are rarely easy, probably extremely difficult to commit to in the moment, but made in the pursuit of a bigger, brighter picture. The thought of going to this wedding was beyond uncomfortable, but was it a reasonable price to invest for another important precedent it would set?

Kate agreed the decision to go or not was up to me, and only I could decide if I could manage it at this point in time. She also highlighted what an opportunity it was to model for ourselves, our kids, our family and friends that we are capable of the kind of uncoupling we want and how we plan to move forward as an expanded family.

"You're right, 'most' divorced people don't do this kind of thing; but I also know you are working with me because you never wanted the divorce 'most' people have," Kate wisely pointed out. "It may feel like faking it, but there's a difference between simply faking something for all the wrong reasons and trying to act in accordance with a new value you've embraced—facilitating a civil and gracious relationship with the father of your kids. There's a steep learning curve there if you want a co-parenting relationship where you and Brandon can attend big life events together, from soccer games and tumbling meets to future graduations and weddings. Many adults have divorced parents who can't even be civil to each other at and for these things. Chances are this is another one of those events you'll never feel 'ready' for, but if you can trust it's a gesture of goodwill, what do you have to lose?"

Right…Ready is a decision, not a feeling.

In hindsight, I am grateful I decided to go, but as you can tell from my journal entry at the time, it was painful. I faked it for my kids and for the bigger picture goal I somehow never lost sight of, and I suppose the moral of this story is that I survived. Even when Brandon's uncle shouted, "Brandon, go get your wife! We're taking pictures!" He wasn't on social media for my announcement, and clearly divorce is an uncomfortable topic to discuss for extended family of divorced couples too. But wow, I was so mad at the situation!

Who, who should I be so mad at? Whose job was that to tell Uncle Dylan that Brandon and Meg are divorced? How dare anyone invite me without having at least told the aunts, uncles, and grandparents that we are no longer married?! I watched from a distance as Brandon jogged across the lawn to him, hurrying to get there before he had a chance to make our kids feel even more awkward. We'd already explained to them how and why Mom wouldn't be in the wedding pictures. Clearly, no one thought to have that same chat with Uncle Dylan. What a mess. Brandon whispered an explanation, and I watched a mortified look cross Dylan's face. I found myself feeling sorry for him; it wasn't his fault he didn't know better and was just trying to include me. But I could only devote so much energy in empathy to that situation before needing to turn away, choking back tears and breathing through some deep, unspeakable sadness that filled every cell of my body as they moved forward with the Campbell family pictures—a family I'd legally dissolved connection to six months ago.

While I remember this being rather traumatic, others in attendance have told me they were impressed with how Brandon and I were able to be at a wedding together; they told me it was refreshing to see a recently divorced couple being not only civil but choosing to share a table, eating and laughing together with their kids. People noticed how wonderful and still happy our kids seemed. Our joint presence and conduct showed everyone what I so badly wanted my kids to feel and come to trust—that we will always be a family.

With Kate's help, I explored the important difference between boundaries and gestures of goodwill, both of which were totally lacking in my marriage (imagine that), but working to figure it out through and post-divorce has been game changing. Boundaries are beautiful, important, necessary things; many a self-help book has been devoted to helping determine and uphold various boundaries with ourselves and others. I won't be diving too much into boundary work here, though I will caution: don't refuse to entertain gestures of goodwill and attribute that refusal/inflexibility to "boundaries." Boundaries are peaceful and powerful, and gestures of goodwill are peaceful and powerful. Refusing to grant a kind gesture that you truly can afford isn't honoring a boundary, it's probably protecting your pride. Learning to recognize the difference is key. However painful those gestures of goodwill seem to make at the time, it's been my experience that they pay you back tenfold. Plus, bonus, you'll likely find you are liking yourself more and more as you lean into that kindness and compassion; it feels way better than withholding grace and goodness. It takes too much precious energy to always be the asshole.

Fantastically Lucky

Fantastically lucky...my theme of the Bear 100 this weekend. I'm fantastically lucky my body can carry me 100 miles, fantastically lucky I get to experience these beautiful mountains and amazing fall colors, fantastically lucky for incredibly supportive family and friends, fantastically lucky for the entire experience.

This race didn't go as planned, few do, I guess. It was mentally and physically difficult, just not in the ways I'd anticipated. I slipped and hurt my knee pretty early on, and by 50 miles, I knew I was either dropping or walking the last half.

The thought of finishing so much slower than I had hoped was beyond discouraging...but then I saw my kids. I didn't know they'd be at Tony Grove (the halfway aid station) and they were so genuinely proud of and excited for me. We've talked a lot about the idea that with any passion they decide to invest time and energy in, it isn't about winning or losing or being the best, it's about showing up and giving it all you've got. Some days that may be way better or faster or prettier than others, but it's the most honest metric of any endeavor. Thank you, Brandon for coming. It made my heart so happy to see you guys, and to know I wasn't done.

I can't say enough about my unbelievable friends who got me through those last 50 miles. They encouraged me, distracted me, made me laugh when I felt like crying, offered trailside massage, kept me moving, told the best stories, read me Cheryl Strayed and Carl Sagan, tended to my disgusting feet, made all sorts of arrangements so they could meet me in the middle of nowhere Bear River mountains, took total care of and were crazy patient with me. I am so lucky to know these amazing humans! And my sweet family and friends sending the kindest words of encouragement...Thank you all!! What a super-humbling, grit-growing, beautifully-painful, epic adventure. So grateful, fantastically lucky! (@megbcampbell September 30, 2018)

Deciding to register, train for, and attempt to run a 100-mile ultramarathon the year of my divorce was up there with my decision to return to graduate school that same fall—questionably sane, at best. But it was also a huge goal that helped me keep my head up. I would run while the kids were gone with Brandon, and I would run when I couldn't stand to be alone in my home. I would run when I needed to move some sad, heavy energy that seemed to lodge in my chest so frequently those days. I suppose running was more of an escape than a self-care practice for a while there; still, a healthier escape than other options I've resorted to in the past.

The Bear 100 is a 100-mile trail race starting in Logan, Utah, and finishing in Fish Haven, Idaho. The course includes over 22,800 feet of vertical gain, moving through the beautiful Bear River Mountains. Logan, Utah, and that mountain range will always occupy a small, happy corner of my heart. Transferring to Utah State at 19 years old marked the end of an era, the end of my competitive Nordic skiing career and the start of that mini-identity crisis number one. I didn't yet understand that lifetimes consist of many eras, many seasons…if you're lucky, anyway.

I loved school, I loved learning, I loved my time in Logan. I came to Utah State so lost, but as luck and the universe and finally doing some self-awareness work would have it, I eventually did find my way. I had the best college roommates with whom I share some of the best college memories. I met Brandon working at a local restaurant—he was a cook, I was a server—and we couldn't stand each other at first. We'd argue over who messed up what orders. I'd for sure indicated no mushrooms in that calzone. He'd insist it wasn't on the ticket. I'd ask about the status of table 83's order, he'd be a smart-ass and reply, "It's being prepared," offering no actual update. I would not have guessed that two years later we'd be camping at Tony Grove together and he'd be proposing to me on Mt. Naomi, the highest peak of the Bear River

Range. Something about the Bear 100 called to me—returning to where it all started—a meeting of the past and present in the context of a race I was sure to suffer, smile, hurt, and grow through. Seemed fitting.

Suffer, smile, hurt, and grow I did, just in ways I didn't anticipate. I was cruising through a downhill section of the course around mile 18, surrounded by beautiful yellow aspen trees, headed toward the next aid station feeling strong and satisfied with my pace. Lost in thought, I slipped on a particularly loose rocky section, and next thing I knew I was mid-fall with the ground fast approaching. I managed to mostly remain on my feet, picking up speed as I scrambled to catch up to the rate I was falling, my right foot catching on a rock, and I ended up sliding in a deep lunge, touching a hand down and majorly straining my hips and knees. Now I'm one of the most inflexible runners you'll ever meet; I haven't sunk into the splits comfortably for decades, so to come this close on accident was painful. It would have probably been better to just go down altogether, hard to say for sure, but scrapes and bruises would have been more welcome than the side effects I started experiencing soon after this "nice save," as the runner behind me complimented.

My knee began hurting after this slip, slowly at first, but by mile 50 it felt like an ice ax was being swung against the outside of my right knee, and this horrible, piercing pain radiated with each step. The only movement that felt bearable was hobbling along, careful to keep my right leg as straight as possible, swearing under my breath whenever I'd momentarily forget and try to take a normal step. If this hadn't been my first 100-miler, if it didn't hold so much symbolism for me personally of surviving what I once believed to be unsurvivable, if it hadn't been this huge goal I'd kept my eye on to distract myself and provide breaks from the divorce heartache, the responsible thing would have been to drop out of the race at mile 50.

I don't want to promote or celebrate pushing through objective injuries. But at the time and under these circumstances, especially once I was surrounded by my kids' invigorating energy and sweet encouragement, I just wasn't ready to drop. I picked up poles at that

Tony Grove aid station. I was able to use them almost as a form of crutches, and at the suggestion of my wise friend and pacer Sara, I simply resolved to get to the next aid station, 10 more miles, then we'd re-evaluate. That is how I mentally tackled the remaining 50 miles—aid station to aid station, just get to the next aid station. I couldn't think about the finish, couldn't let myself focus on the knee pain, couldn't dwell on how much farther, how much longer, how very slow I was moving. I just focused on getting to the next aid station.

The first 50 miles I completed in under 14 hours, and the next 50 took me over 20 hours to hobble through. Occasionally the thought would cross my mind, *This is so miserable*, especially freezing through the middle of the night when I couldn't run to stay warm, or the final downhill miles to the finish (downhill was the hardest on my knee) when everyone and their dog was passing me. Still, I couldn't deny this was nothing compared to the extreme discomfort of divorce the past year.

I'd learn the following week that I'd partially dislocated my hip, and the displacement was resulting in debilitating knee pain. Crazy how easy it is to sometimes misunderstand the source of a problem, or misattribute it altogether. After the race my symptoms remained impossible to ignore. I'd been icing my knee and rolling my quads, hamstrings, and IT bands daily; I even got an X-ray confirming my knee joint and bones looked fine.

What the hell? I thought. *Nothing is fine when I can't run or hardly walk.* Turns out I just needed someone to think to look up—literally *look up* my leg—realize the problem was my hip and adjust it back into place. I couldn't see it, couldn't even think it because I was so focused on the acute pain in my knee. I hobbled into that appointment miserable, walked out pain-free and marveling at more running-pain-divorce analogies.

I did plenty of misunderstanding and misattributing in my marriage. I think that's common by the end of many marriages. We're trying to treat symptoms, often unaware of what the actual and underlying causes and problems even are, so focused on and resentful of present pain. Divorce ultimately allowed me to look up, to finally broaden my view of the state of my marriage at its end and reasons for its demise. And isn't that the hope of any uncoupling, any change, any transition in life—that we've gained a deeper understanding of ourselves, learned something, can move forward transformed by not only the pain but by our willingness to look up and work to understand the cause and our role in all of it? How fantastically lucky we are for the chance to suffer, smile, hurt, and grow through the seasons we're granted.

On the other side of this sentiment, how wasteful to refuse to look up, to instead bury your head, dig in your heels, pick the pettiest of battles. Divorce is a long damn process with side effects that'll need revisiting and resolving for a long damn time. I don't say this to be negative or discouraging, but to hopefully help manage some expectations and keep perspective.

Whether I'm running 5 miles, 50, or 100, I am spent and done at the finish; I couldn't run another step because both mentally and physically I've planned to be done at that distance. There's no such precision planning or timing with divorce, we can only count on it being an ultramarathon of countless ups and downs. Don't get fixated on or try to plan too much for the finish, just move from aid station to aid station; many days this'll be minute to minute, as best you can, and trust that you are moving toward the happiest you've ever been, toward your most whole self. When you find yourself turning ugly, mean, or bitter, look up and redirect.

Proof Points

Half a year after the Bear, a friend (and also ultra running coach) would refer to my Bear endeavor as a proof point. I was debating whether I'd ever do a 100-miler again when he expressed not only belief that I could finish another, but complete one strong and competitively. When I pushed back, still feeling a little sorry for myself and wondering aloud if that distance just "isn't for me," he maintained that finishing the Bear under the circumstances I did proves it can be done, and I can compete in 100s. I needn't question whether I'm capable or belong.

When others generously comment that they're impressed with Brandon and my divorce but feel they could never do that or maintain it'd be impossible for them or that there's just no way, let our divorce— let any seemingly amicable divorce you've witnessed or read of or heard about—be your proof point. They're out there! I understand it's tempting to assume those divorces were somehow immune from incredibly difficult circumstances; they weren't. I've mentioned deep hurt permeated every aspect and every second of our lives during those dark divorce days, but I will say (again, always excluding instances involving abuse), intentionally choosing and living a gracious, conscious uncoupling can be done, regardless of varying individual and "impossible" circumstances.

I don't say this self-righteously or with any judgment; I simply refuse to downplay or minimize our pain, our process, our work. And I no longer engage with anyone wishing to debate that our divorce was "easy." Anyone dismissing or trying to explain away proof points is working hard to maintain some victim status (when it's unwarranted), determined to profit off a divorce (money, property, custody, etc.) no matter the damage, desperate to protect and feed a fragile ego, and/or the thought of surrendering to a new season is simply too much, too hard. So they resist, deny, fight, and ultimately perpetuate a lot of hurt in the process.

With nearly half of marriages ending in divorce, I don't think anyone is lacking for anecdotal evidence surrounding the construct. I've heard plenty of stories, followed divorces of parents of my students, watched from a distance many a neighbor or acquaintance divorce, been there for close friends of my own navigating the end of marriages, and more recently, I have had total strangers reaching out seeking support through a divorce. I agree that it's less common to observe former partners cooperate civilly through the divorce process. If you're one of these rare instances where you and your former spouse are willing and able to divorce collaboratively, possibly with the help of a mediator and/or minimal lawyer involvement, you're one of the lucky ones! Don't take this for granted; genuinely thank and appreciate each other, even if you can't stand each other.

Nearly six years post-divorce, I was listening to divorce attorney James Sexton on Lex Fridman's podcast discussing marriage, divorce, and relationships. I was surprised to find myself crying happy tears at hearing him share advice he gives divorcing parents in his office.

> I say this to clients, they got a four-year-old, they're getting divorced. There's going to be a wedding, in like 20-something years, there's going to be a wedding. And, it's either going to be the wedding where they got to put these people on opposite sides of the room cause if they pass each other by the shrimp boat they're going to kill each other, or it's the wedding where you stand there, you take some pictures, you kinda go like, 'yeah, we fucked up this whole marriage thing, but man we did a good job with this kid, didn't we?' You know, and the decisions you make right now, there's a straight line to that wedding. (Sexton 2023)

I have a co-parent who values that line, who is aware and kind, who grants gestures of goodwill, and refuses to ever detract from choosing and celebrating our kids because they let animosity consume them. I acknowledge Brandon and I are more the exception than the rule here, and I'm deeply grateful.

In other instances of divorce, I've observed one person remain grounded while the other spirals. My heart breaks for individuals who are capable of a conscious uncoupling but can't control the conduct of a partner who is either unwilling or unable to meet them in that gracious space. I'm in awe of these individuals striving to live in line with a personal code of kind and reasonable conduct, even when their former partner has grown intolerably cruel and vindictive. For anyone finding themselves in this situation, I'm so sorry. The only way out is through, and with a ton of boundaries. (Boundaries are essential for dealing with unreasonable people and erratic behavior. You'll want and need both a therapist and a lawyer to help with those boundaries.)

Don't hang on to the hope for a gracious uncoupling while the more irrational spouse ruins the family financially or subjects your kids to unsettling and unnecessary time in limbo land. Sadly, your hope for a more amicable divorce is unlikely to deter or redirect anyone on a warpath. You can't reason someone into or out of a position they didn't arrive at with reason to begin with, and "reasonable" isn't the default for most individuals going through divorce. Those determined to numb and run from the pain of their own making will remain in this vicious cycle, working to suck in anyone trying to break free. It's not fair or excusable, but it's the reality many individuals endure far too long trying to uncouple from someone incapable of taking accountability and/or letting go.

I can only imagine how horribly painful it'd be to watch your child be manipulated by their other parent, to watch your child be used as a tool to hurt you as much as possible, to be threatened with the idea of not seeing your child. If I ever thought my divorce was the ultimate surrender, it's certainly a distant second to this scenario that plays out too often. Focus on what is within your control and invest in resources necessary to pursue what's fair and best for your family. It will take years for kids to unpack and process their experience of this kind of divorce—another unfair and inexcusable outcome largely outside your influence and with the potential to drive you absolutely crazy. If you can remain a stable, loving, authoritative parent in your kids' lives through all this, I wholeheartedly believe there will come a day when they are able to more objectively recognize the various roles both parents played through this bumpy chapter, and they'll be appreciative of yours.

Many people stay married for years, lifetimes even, to avoid long, nasty divorces they aren't convinced they could protect their kids through. I understand this justification for remaining married. It wasn't my reality, but I know it's others, and honestly, I can't say what I'd choose if I ever had to wonder or worry my former spouse would put our kids in the middle of a virulent divorce. That's a crippling corner to be backed into. If you're reading this and it resonates, I'm sending all the patient, brave, wise, and resolved energy your way. Not sure I'd be able to leave that corner myself, but I have been privileged to observe other courageous souls move forward with hope in a happier future, obtain necessary support, embrace the action and change that choosing truth and authenticity requires. I have watched them become another's proof point (particularly their children's) that it's important to break toxic cycles once you recognize them, that joy and wholeness are worth moving and working toward.

Dates

> After a while you learn the subtle difference
> Between holding a hand and chaining a soul,
> And you learn that love doesn't mean leaning
> And company doesn't mean security,
> And you begin to learn that kisses aren't contracts
> And presents aren't promises,
> And you begin to accept your defeats
> With your head up and your eyes open
> With the grace of a woman, not the grief of a child,
> And you learn to build all your roads on today,
> Because tomorrow's ground is too uncertain for plans,
> And futures have a way of falling down in mid-flight.
> After a while you learn
> That even sunshine burns if you get too much.
> So you plant your own garden and decorate your own soul,
> Instead of waiting for someone to bring you flowers.
> You learn that you really can endure…
> That you really are strong,
> And you really do have worth.
> And you learn and learn…
> With every goodbye you learn. (Shoffstall 1971)

It's been seven months since Brandon and I got divorced. It still feels really recent, even though plenty of days in between have felt like eternities. Today we would have celebrated our 12th anniversary. Like most post-divorce firsts, this is a rough

123

one. I'm going to talk about it, because we tend not to and I think we should. Pretending to be more okay than we are doesn't help us heal faster, nor does it honor our reasons for grieving in the first place.

I remain forever grateful for the friend and amazing co-parent I have in Brandon. We've both learned things about ourselves and grown in ways we never could or would have without this experience. But it's hard, some days more than others. There have been many bright and happy moments, and there's also been lots of crying on my bathroom floor.

But of all the things I've learned this past year, I believe this: everything expressed in this poem is key. Trying to keep my head up, eyes open, practicing gratitude, choosing love, doing the soul work and remembering that real life moves forward and in the direction of our intentions because "time doesn't heal us, we do" (Thomas 2016). (@megbcampbell October 4, 2018)

It's fascinating what dates hold significance for us and why. It's so personal. October 17, June 1, June 3—those were just days the first 25, 27, and 30 years of my life. Then, the birth of a baby made those dates among the most meaningful and significant of my whole existence. We keep track of major life events with dates, sort life phases into befores and afters. There's before and after the kids, before and after the death of a loved one, before and after a divorce. Where Brandon and I used to celebrate the start of our marriage on October 4, we now wish each other "Happy Divorciversary" every March 16.

After a while, I've found neither October 4 nor March 16 sting the way they used to. It's hard to imagine at first, but the significance of once-difficult dates evolve with you.

Happy side story...This "After a While" poem was first recommended to me somewhere in the expansive land of social media. I saved and shared with my own thoughts (the Instagram caption quoted above) on my first un-anniversary. Years later (on my 38th birthday), I opened my mailbox to find a letter from my sweet Grandma. Knowing how difficult it was for her to write, her fine motor control deteriorating with age, made her kind words all the more meaningful. She wrote of how grateful she is for her life, her family, for me, for her great-grandkids. She shared how much she missed her husband who passed away over 13 years ago, mere months before Jude (the first great-grandchild) was born. I remember that goodbye well, watching my Granddad's physical body expire at the same time I could feel Jude's growing within me, very aware and in awe of the intense fragility and brilliance of life.

Teary eyed I pulled out a newspaper clipping she'd referenced in her letter. I began reading: "The author of 'Comes the Dawn' is Veronica A. Shoffstall, N.Y.C.," and below was the same poem I'd shared on Instagram back in 2018. The piece of newspaper was old but appeared carefully saved, yellowed in color, thin and uncreased. Referencing an ad for Rocky Mountain Gardening (printed on the opposite side of the poem), I assume my Grandma came across this in the mid-1970s, while living in Frisco, Colorado.

Tears streamed down my face as I marveled at the power of written language to transcend generations, at my Grandma's still sharp mind, at the interconnectedness I can't explain but am so grateful to feel. My 85-year-old Grandma recognized what I shared on social media, retrieved a rectangular piece of newspaper she'd cut out 40-something years ago, and mailed it to me. A poem that resonated with her in the '70s went on to speak to me over four decades later; both of us compelled to save the wisdom in those lines, just in different mediums.

An internet search will populate countless instances of this poem, conflicting origin stories, and various titles ("After a While," "Comes the Dawn," "You Learn")—in the references list of this account I cite "Comes the Dawn," from the newspaper clipping saved then shared with me by my beloved Grandma.

PART 4

2019

Rising

The irony is that we attempt to disown our difficult stories to appear more whole or more acceptable, but our wholeness—even our wholeheartedness—actually depends on the integration of all of our experiences, including the falls. (Brown 2015, 38)

I started 2019 with a few freezing, beautiful miles, and lots of thoughts.

If you know me well, I've probably (perhaps obnoxiously) insisted on talking about Brene Brown's ideas at one point or another. For how obsessed I've been with her work for years, I've put off reading *Rising Strong*. I think I'm getting better at owning the real, I can wrap my mind around the importance of choosing courage over comfort, and I feel more compassion and genuine empathy for the entire human experience than ever before…But the resilient part, the getting up again after each fall, especially when some falls in the big arenas feel like life-defining failures…that's freaking hard.

Like all of her books, I knew the wisdom in this one would be both important and scary—like how the struggle, the heavy, the unpacking and facing hurt (both experienced and caused), the dark middle step, the work of healing before eventually rising—no one gets to skip that step. And of course, I knew I was no exception, just needed a minute (which turned into a year) to half-ignore the difficult story while navigating survival mode…2018 has been a crazy chapter, and now this *Rising Strong* is kind of kicking my butt, but in a good way.

Thank you to everyone who continues to show up for, love, and support me. I imagine a lot of relationships have felt very one-sided lately; please know I appreciate you. I love you, and I am sorry and will do better. I know falling and rising over and over and over again is the work of living, and I'm so grateful to begin another year on this spectacular pale blue dot. Here's to hopefully making some progress toward rising strong in 2019. Happy New Year! (@megbcampbell January 1, 2019)

January first. Another date forever with its own significance for pretty much everyone. As a kid and young adult, I lived in a lot of excited anticipation for the next "big" thing; I had really no concept of living presently until my thirties. When I did start learning about the notion, largely through Eckhart Tolle's *The Power of Now* (1997) and *A New Earth* (2005) books, the content presented was super difficult for me to make sense of at first, then also pretty life-changing once I did. I embraced the practice of trying to live more in the now almost overnight because it felt so obvious, so important, so good.

Throughout 2018, the year of my divorce, full of so much fallout and heartache, there was this ever-present tension between longing for a new someday when everything wasn't so damn hard and sad all the time, while also trying to honor my commitment of remaining present, feeling every step, owning and integrating the dark middle. A couple of friends who'd lived the experience of divorce before me had shared some insight that, while divorce will be the hardest thing you've ever done, you're also about a year away from the happiest you've ever been. I doubted that probability often the first year, but in hindsight have decided I mostly agree. The year is a rough estimate, and "happiest you've ever been" only applies if you're willing to do the work, willing to explore your role, including the falls and failures, then actively rise.

127

Inevitability and Forgiveness

> We have all hurt someone tremendously, whether by intent or accident. We have all loved someone tremendously, whether by intent or accident. It is an intrinsic human trait, and a deep responsibility, I think, to be an organ and a blade. But learning to forgive ourselves and others because we have not chosen wisely is what makes us most human. We make horrible mistakes. It's how we learn. We breathe love. It's how we learn. And it is inevitable. (Waheed, n.d.)

This remains one of my favorite reminders—but I had no idea how much forgiveness work I had ahead when I first came across and saved this thought. Five years later, I can wrap my mind and practice around forgiving others. The idea of forgiving myself still feels abstract.

Perhaps it's simply surrendering to the reality that I've made poor choices, caused myself and others pain, and altered trajectories in irreversible ways; then using these understandings as a catalyst for growth, and ultimately releasing those versions of me who didn't know better or weren't brave enough to do better in the past.

Toward the end of 2022 I watched *Stutz*, the documentary by Jonah Hill (2022) exploring various tools he learned from his therapist Phil Stutz. Like many viewers, I grew rather fond of Phil Stutz. He exudes gentleness while also calling out the bullshit. The tools and insights he shares are powerful. I was especially struck by his outline of three inevitable things no one can escape: pain, uncertainty, and constant work. I couldn't help but marvel at the irony, how much heartache would have been avoided and suffering actually lessened (instead of caused) if I'd just understood and accepted earlier that pain, uncertainty, and work were inescapable conditions of existence, versus things to manically try and avoid.

That's the Hope

> Darling, you deserve it all. You deserve love and peace and magic and joy dancing in your eyes. You deserve hearty, deep-

belly laughter and the right to let those tears fall and water the soil. You deserve freedom and *goodness* and company and days of bliss and quiet too. You deserve you happy and healed and content and open. So, keep going, darling. Keep going. Go realize into being the life you deserve. (Anonymous 2018)

Happy and healed and content and open, that's the hope. And that's all it was at the time, a distant hope. At first, it felt wrong to even allow myself hope in such "selfish" things. Later, when I could not yet imagine "happy and healed and content and open," but wanted to, I tried to start hoping more actively. Hope is powerful, a dynamic energy source that fuels healing. Hope is key to taking that next step, doing the next right thing. But how to cultivate hope? Many days, despair was much more tempting to grasp at. Plus, it seemed to come in waves. I'd be doing well, feeling optimistic, focused on growth, motivated to do the work; then I'd slip into major sadness, be guilt-ridden over past choices all over again, and feel deep despair over my life not looking how I thought it would or should.

It's wild how easy it is to succumb to the negative spiraling, to drown in the darkness some days. I'm still figuring out how to better navigate these waves, but what I've come up with so far is that hope doesn't necessarily or always feel natural; it's something we need to intentionally practice. Below I've compiled suggestions, things that have supported me in both holding and growing hope:

Practice coping strategies when things are going well.

I've read many a self-help book, listened to countless podcasts, studied mindfulness, and worked with therapists and coaches. I have some tried-and-true tools. (If you are thinking you don't, that is where you start. And good news, there are amazing resources out there!) Still, being familiar with what works for me isn't enough. I practice these things when I'm calm and in my upstairs, rational brain so when that fight-flight-freeze response is triggered, when I'm flooded with big emotions, I have the "muscle/mental memory" to still employ a coping strategy, to self-soothe and regulate.

Metacognition refers to our ability to think about our thoughts.

We are not our thoughts, we are the observer of our thoughts. How amazing is that?! It's how and why, when we better hone this skill of observing, we can recognize how our thoughts affect how we feel, how we act, how we interact with the world around us.

In the helping professions, we learn about stages of change: precontemplation, contemplation, preparation, action, and maintenance (Prochaska, Johnson, and Lee 2009). You could present someone with the most-likely-to-be-effective tools ever, but they'd be rather useless if that person wasn't ready and/or didn't recognize a need for change.

I went to my first appointment with a therapist in my early twenties at the suggestion of my parents. I was young and dumb, skeptical as ever because I ignorantly figured I'd figure it out myself. I was in the contemplation stage (aware of problems but not convinced I needed to change, certainly not yet ready to change), trying to force action (the stage where you do the work, address the problems), and you simply can't skip or force progression through those stages. I remember this therapist drawing a triangle, labeling each corner "thoughts," "feelings," "behavior" and explaining how they interact with and affect each other, particularly how if we focus on changing our thoughts it will start to change how we feel, and ultimately, act. I had just finished my undergraduate degree in psychology and remember arrogantly thinking, *No shit, what a waste of time.* I didn't return for a second session.

I wasn't ready to understand or embrace the depth of that seemingly simple triangle. Change your thoughts, change your self-talk, change the climate of your mind; shifts in these things can absolutely change your life. I now find visualizing Dr. Dan Siegel's (2021) Wheel of Awareness particularly helpful. In this analogy, the hub of the wheel is our center, our core. Here we are aware, open and receptive, calm and at peace. This is where we want to operate from as often as possible. The rim of the wheel represents countless areas where we can focus our attention; it's often easy to get stuck on the rim. Sometimes this is helpful. For example, if you've broken your ankle, getting stuck on that sensation of pain will ensure you obtain medical attention and get the help you need. Other times we get stuck on rather unproductive or even harmful thoughts, feelings, or perceptions. (Like *how awful my ex is* or *how bad divorce sucks* or *how unjust life is*. It's risky to remain stuck on these spots.)

We, however, have the ability to return to the hub, our calm center, then redirect our focus and attention elsewhere. With my own kids and students, once they're familiar with this analogy, we just refer to it as "needing to spin our wheel" anytime we're stuck. When I'm really down and struggling to find a safer, gentler space on the rim, I can always return to and simply focus on my breath—a grounding tool that's always there and able to help return me to the hub.

Pick up a shovel.

Shera has yet another stellar analogy I can't help but reference any time I'm discussing stages of change. Most of us, at one time or another, have been irritated to step outside our residence and find someone else's dog has shit on our front lawn or sidewalk. For some, the obvious course of action is to grab a bag or shovel and simply pick it up. Others will whine and complain and seek external confirmation of just how unacceptable this is; the injustice of it all distracts them from problem solving, and before long they've gone and stepped in the pile.

Instead of acknowledging (contemplation, preparation stages) and addressing (action) the issue, they lament how they're now covered in crap, how it's not their fault, and why they feel owed assistance in cleaning up. If this cycle continues, when these individuals go to seek support from shovel-wielding friends (especially if those friends value boundaries that protect their peace), they're soon relegated to front-porch acquaintances: "I'm sorry, you can't come in, you're covered in crap." Unable to recognize these friends opted to pick up instead of perpetuate a mess, they start to resent them for having less shit to deal with, better circumstances, easier lives.

We're all faced with different hardships, different piles of proverbial dog poop placed in our paths that we have to figure out how to handle, how to clean up. Take accountability when it's a mess of your own making, be proactive and problem solve when it's a mess you inherit—use a shovel and resolve to remain uncovered in crap!

Practice more self-compassion.

I've mentioned I'm a big fan of self-compassion. It isn't toxic positivity, it doesn't feel like lying to yourself, it's not affirmation statements. Those surely have a place in healing, growth, and goal setting but often feel painfully incongruent when you're in a dark space. Self-compassion is showing yourself unconditional love and acceptance, even—and especially—at your lowest points. Compassionate self-talk is a great place to spin your wheel, direct your focus; engaging in it is likely to change how you feel, even elicit some hope.

Remember hard feelings are part of a happy life.

When I'm having a hard time breaking out of a low funk, I literally have to remind and ask myself things like: *Your brain is doing what brains do, trying to protect you, but it's lying to you right now...Feelings aren't facts...Are you assigning truth to these thoughts?...I feel sad/overwhelmed/ frustrated* (name the feeling)... *Give this big emotion 90 seconds, where do you feel it in your body? Let it move... You are doing your best... You are safe... What do you need right now?...Let's go for a run!* Hard feelings are part of a happy life and will inevitably come and go; don't resist them. Instead, focus on taking good care of yourself through them.

Prioritizing foundational physical-health needs will set you up for success. Be sure you are drinking enough water, getting enough sleep, fueling your mind and body with foods that help you feel your best, moving your body regularly, and engaging in nervous system regulation practices. (The physiological sigh, meditation, breath work—look up "voo breathing" to stimulate branches of the vagus nerve—my therapist-sister Erika recently introduced me to this technique and it's one of my new favorites!)

Cultivate a marvel mindset.

I was listening to another Lex Fridman podcast with guest Paul Conti in early 2023, during the editing stages of this book. Dr. Conti is a psychiatrist whose holistic view of individuals, trauma, cultures, and systems intrigues me. In the beginning of this episode, they discuss concepts of time, physics of the universe, entropy and counter-entropy, an underlying creative force, if atoms know love or not. So fascinating!

Conti points out how fantastically improbable our existence is, and we don't often give conscious attention to this complexity. "We don't think about that, how we're in the middle of something so vast and built on top of so many layers. I think it leads us to be cavalier with human life, including often our own." He goes on to recount starting medical school, showing up expecting to learn and better understand so much; what he discovered, though, is just how complex the human brain, body, behavior, and our collective existence truly is. "I think the more we know about us, the more we respectfully marvel."

Fridman agrees, "We should proactively marvel at every layer." If we were better at this, we'd be a lot less likely to find and get stuck on things we don't like about ourselves and others. We'd be less driven by scarcity, less drawn to hurt and destroy, and more aligned with abundance, creativity, and love.

To marvel is to be filled with wonder or astonishment. This existence surely warrants marveling. Marvel at the uniqueness of snowflakes, the sun warming your face on a smooth piece of slickrock, the color of your child's eyes, the countless complicated and life-sustaining processes happening involuntarily in you every moment of every day. At any given minute you could pause and find something to marvel at: the light hitting your eyes right now, electrical impulses traveling your optic nerve to your brain, where these signals are translated to images—images you've learned to recognize, read, and make meaning of. (We could get into other layers here. If you can see, are literate, have the time for leisure reading—all these facts point to a privileged position.)

In trying to articulate my thoughts here, I kept reaching for a different word, a synonym to marveling with a less positive connotation…perhaps shock, disbelief? Something about marveling at suffering, devastation, evil, and pain doesn't sound quite right, yet we certainly wonder at and are astonished by the dark and hard stuff too. We marvel at the capacity for evil in this world, wonder at the rhyme or reason behind deep hurt, feel astonished by the debilitating ache of a broken heart. As I'm editing this section (February 2023), the world is watching in disbelief at the devastation currently observable in Turkey and Syria from recent earthquakes, feeling small and insignificant when compared to the layers that are physical tectonic plates capable of such destruction.

The practice of marveling, whatever end of the spectrum I find myself participating in day to day—whether it's in regard to something unique and magical or terrifying and tragic—it's a mindset that reliably serves to both humble and provide better perspective. I hope we'll continue to marvel at the intricacies of this existence, and also marvel at the power and importance of hope throughout it.

More Hard Questions

Coming up on a year post-divorce, so also been almost a year since we were last in Sun Valley. Can't help but remember the impossible heaviness Brandon and I were feeling that trip, and the crazy difference a year has made. Back then I wasn't sure we'd ever be here all together again. We get asked a lot about our co-parenting relationship and navigating a new friendship. I'm going to talk about it (again), because I do believe that story is our way home.

I'm sharing (and with Brandon's permission) a few thoughts from this weekend. At the risk of sounding a little/a lot dramatic, this past year was hell. There were days I couldn't imagine things would ever feel better or lighter or even remotely okay; but here we are, on the other side of a lot of hurt and heartache and figuring out a new normal.

How are Brandon and I able to still spend time together? Our kids. Forever sharing, raising, loving and being so completely invested in their well-being—that's powerful. Also, the conscious uncoupling philosophy; this idea that two people can leave a romantic relationship graciously, with kindness and gratitude for all that was experienced and created together. After 14 years we made some big changes, but couldn't imagine not remaining in each other's lives.

Why not just stay married if you get along? We know this question well. Truth is, we did stay married for a long time because it was "good enough." But both Brandon and I couldn't grow in the box that was our marriage. We were stuck, both getting small, dim, colder. I still believe only the two people who make up a marriage can know when to hold on or move on…Marriage is hard, divorce is hard…You choose your hard, and for us this was the right decision. Our kids see a much healthier dynamic between their parents now. Brandon and I both feel lighter, more hopeful and more authentic, finding the versions of us we want our kids to know.

There's been lots of work and intention and mistakes and amends—still figuring it out one day at a time; forever grateful we're a family! (@megbcampbell February 24, 2019)

This post was scary to share. Over the course of our first year divorced, people had tons of questions for Brandon and me with regard to our post-marriage conduct and relationship. Some were complimentary and curious, others were skeptical and critical. The questions haven't stopped, but my comfort level with answering has increased over the years. At the time, the questions I addressed in this post were the most common and dang intimidating. Brandon and I didn't know what we were doing or exactly why all the time—just moving day to day, trying to honor those joint intentions of protecting the kids, not turning ugly, making small gestures of goodwill when we could muster the strength and humility, figuring out and shaping a new normal as we went.

I remember worrying we were "doing it wrong," as if there's one and only one way to live through and after divorce. Occasionally I would wonder about what others thought, what gossip was circulating, if Brandon's truck was in my driveway too often, if us still vacationing together was too weird. I didn't know exactly what I was doing at the time—Martha Beck and Glennon Doyle (2022) gave me the words for it in a podcast episode years later—but I was simply moving toward what felt warm. It felt warm to be kind to my kids' dad, it felt warm to encourage their love and admiration of him, it felt warm to invite him to dinner some nights, it felt warm to spend Christmas morning together, it felt warm to still take spontaneous desert trips to southern Utah or ski trips to Sun Valley together.

Then I'd feel a pang of self-doubt or even embarrassment when people would make comments like, "I couldn't stand to be around my ex that much," "Why not stay married? You're acting married," or "Do you ever worry if you're confusing your kids?" That potentially-confusing-the-kids suggestion was the most triggering; everything we were doing was with the ultimate goal of supporting our kids, trying to hold as much of this as possible for them, not asking them to suffer more than necessary for a decision and the resulting change they had no say or control over. Had we missed the mark and were somehow making it worse?

I brought this up with Brandon, asking if he thought we were confusing them. "Should we try to stick to a more traditional custody schedule? Should we not all hang out together as often? Maybe you should start coming to the front door instead of through the garage? Are we hurting the kids?!"

Now I've heard varying descriptions of Brandon's more defining temperament and personality traits: from confident and calm (especially under pressure), intelligent, hardworking and trustworthy, to absent-minded, unemotional, even aloof. He's brilliant, occasionally lost deep in thought…he's creative, flexible, and impressively present in his day-to-day life (among the least phone-addicted adults I know!)…he's also loyal and brutally honest. He loves physically and mentally challenging adventures, from paragliding to rock climbing to ski mountaineering (I think his stable headspace lends itself to excelling in these activities). He loves big if you've won his big love, he's also picky about his people. Something I've come to understand well about Brandon over the past 20 years is that he's very pragmatic; logic and critical thinking are core values. He's willing to question and explore his perception and understanding of everything, striving to proactively participate and live in objective reality—he's passionate about what is honest, what is real, what is kind. He's incredibly patient when/where he's deemed patience is warranted, he's also not slow or afraid to point out and address the nonsense.

I can't tell you how many times in our marriage various expressions of these traits drove me crazy. At times I would feel unseen, ignored, invalidated. All things we could have worked on had we had any tools to understand the dynamic and to communicate effectively years earlier, but that's neither here nor there now. In and after our divorce, however, this characteristic—Brandon's straightforward directness—has been such a gift.

"I've thought about this a lot," he began answering. "I just can't imagine a future where our kids ever come to think or feel: *My parents got divorced when I was young, then they were nice to each other, they were always cordial and able to both attend and celebrate my big milestones, I never had to mediate awkward encounters of my divorced parents, we still hung out and made memories as a family...It was the worst.*" I smile and roll my eyes at his sarcasm, but it's resonating. "Our kids will have plenty to fault us for," he continued. "But loving them so much that we figured out how to co-parent really well, I just can't find any way or reason to believe that's a bad thing."

That's when I gave myself permission to keep shaping and living my dream divorce. I don't care if it's unconventional, I don't care what anyone else thinks, I don't even stress over the questions my kids may or may not have one day; we'll cross those bridges as they come. I care about turning toward what feels warm. I care about intentionally directing my accountability; I am accountable to myself and my kids, trying to ensure my conduct reflects my deepest values, hopes, and dreams. Family is a core value, these kids are my dream, and I'm beyond hopeful for enduring and authentic relationships with them. I don't feel that doing divorce this way compromises those things, but instead enhances them.

Plus, they get to see both their parents grow and glow and thrive in ways that just weren't possible while married. Perhaps in a perfect world, my kids' parents would be madly in love with each other, able to problem solve any conflict, grow together in the same direction and at the same pace. But that wasn't our relationship, and that's okay. Choosing to live in reality was acknowledging our marriage was a mess, that we were forcing it, that it was dishonest and lonely. I continue to believe that choosing divorce was brave; it was hopeful, it was modeling for our kids the importance of acknowledging what is and building the life we want from there, versus living in denial and waiting on a dream that reality never acknowledges.

Years after this Sun Valley post, while participating in a course for working moms with life coach and good friend Katy Blommer (more on this to come!), Katy imparted wisdom that majorly applies to anyone also fielding questions about their conduct during/after divorce, or really any time ever, for that matter. Don't take advice or offense or anything to heart from someone whose life you wouldn't want. Don't give their unsolicited opinions your time and energy. It's funny how sensitive I was to others' input, but when it came down to it, the people making me most uncomfortable about my own divorce were people I wouldn't trade life choices or values or circumstances with. Remembering this helps me acknowledge but also quickly dismiss any unconstructive feedback I receive about myself, my choices, my divorce, and my life.

On the other hand (because playing devil's advocate can be productive), if a typically reasonable, genuine, and trustworthy friend tries to illuminate a blind spot...be open to their observations, listen. Chances are they're trying to help you see aspects of reality you've perhaps overlooked, and doing so from a place of wanting to see you succeed. It's a balance—the whole not caring what others think/say/believe practice and the possibility you may be in the wrong. Openness is key. Therapists, coaches, and bedroom friends are instrumental in pointing out places you've assigned truth to feelings or perceptions that need re-evaluating. I've been the fortunate recipient of such magnanimous intervention, and I'm grateful to those willing to risk uncomfortable conversations in order to support my overarching hopes and goals.

Buckskin Gulch

I knew these kids were tough, but wow, this trip was hands-down the hardest thing we've ever done. I've done Buckskin as a long day trip with girlfriends and have wanted to take kids back ever since. I was psyched to get permits to backpack it this summer when I thought it'd be plenty dry. When I called the visitor center the day before leaving (for an update on conditions in the canyon), I was told there were a "handful of ankle deep pools."

Um, seriously confused at the miscommunication there because we must have crossed at least 25 pools ranging from ankle to chest deep. I can't believe how much water was down there! We decided to carry our kids across the pools because they would have gotten dangerously cold, so each pool involved Brandon and I making multiple trips to get packs and kids across. Pool miles were crazy slow, my heart sank every time we turned a corner and saw another one. Kids hiked 11 miles that first day but were on their feet for 13 hours! The rock jam also proved way more challenging than anticipated. Brandon ended up lowering me, the kids, and packs down a 20 ft drop before down-climbing a sketchy section to meet up with us.

We also saw a dead mountain goat that'd fallen into the canyon (sad and scary because now I need to worry about falling goats), several scorpions, one tarantula, and a dead rattlesnake that still managed to super-spook me and I proceeded to constantly remind our kids to watch out for them. I am shocked at how awesome of attitudes everyone had…Exhaustion, extreme temperatures (from freezing in the canyon to ridiculously hot in Paria wash), wet sandy shoes and clothes, heavy packs…These are circumstances that can bring out the worst sometimes, and we all managed to stay positive and calm.

I'm especially grateful for Brandon; truly couldn't ask for a more supportive co-parent and friend. We never could have gotten kids through the longest known slot canyon IN THE WORLD without each other—feeling lucky we still want to adventure together as a family.

Also, no one is in a hurry to go back. Story said maybe when she's 26, Violet called us bad parents for taking her there, and Jude is simply calling it "memorable." (@megbcampbell July 6, 2019)

This was another family adventure I never thought I'd see come to fruition; I couldn't have guessed back in January of 2018 Brandon and I would one day reach a place where we could move our family safely through Buckskin Gulch together. Buckskin is an impressive slot canyon in southern Utah. The canyon itself is about 13 miles long, with sandstone rock walls towering about 400 feet tall at the canyon's deepest point. For most of those 13 miles, the canyon floor is no more than 10 feet wide. Once in the canyon, there is only one option for a still-strenuous exit at about mile 8, in case of an emergency like a potential flash flood, injury, dehydration, etc. It's inherently dangerous to pass through and requires a great deal of preparation, canyoneering and hiking experience, some backcountry navigation skills, and clear weather. Buckskin is the longest and deepest slot canyon in the US, possibly the longest in the world, as far as I can tell from a quick internet search. Extreme temperatures (from boiling hot during the approach and exit to frigid pools and chilling temps deep in the canyon), long time on your feet, and one rock jam to descend presented the biggest challenges this trip.

I'd done Buckskin with my girlfriends a couple of years earlier as a birthday trip adventure. Susie was particularly terrified of the pools and resulting cold, reminding me only my birthday wish would get her there. She would go on to later compare her experience of Buckskin to my divorce.

"This is a lot like that time we hiked Buckskin Gulch," she said, referencing how my divorce was unfolding. "It's so dark, so miserable, so cold, no light or end in sight…You want to cry at every new pool, not knowing what to expect, never knowing when it'll get better…You can't feel your lower body, can't stop the uncontrollable shivering, you're convinced you may very possibly die. But you keep going, you eventually turn a corner and there's the smallest sliver of bright, warm sunlight… Your teeth slowly stop chattering, you start to thaw out, you realize you're going to be okay. You look up and notice the beauty all around. And in the end, you decide it was worth it."

Not wanting to invalidate her experience of my birthday Buckskin trip, I mostly managed to hold back my giggles. "Whoa, I'm sorry that was so traumatic for you," I teased. We still laugh about this Buckskin-divorce analogy years later. "Remember that one time Susie practically got divorced, when we made her do Buckskin?!"

Just like I wouldn't have guessed my family would all return to Sun Valley post-divorce, I had no way of knowing and very little reason to hope we'd be tackling Buckskin as a family in the future. I know, I know—we are fortunate for such post-divorce circumstances. But I also know Brandon and I had a lot to do with creating this good fortune, and it didn't happen overnight. I like to think of this trip as the result of over a year's worth of small gestures of goodwill, over a year's worth of leaning into discomfort, being vulnerable and intentional about healing, a year's worth of turning toward warmth and shaping the post-divorce and co-parenting relationship we wanted.

Our kids were 6, 9, and 10 years old on this trip. I look back at these Buckskin pictures and can't believe how little they were, especially surrounded by towering canyon walls. They all carried their own packs of varying sizes, individually heavy in relation to their own bodies. When we'd reach a good stopping spot for water and food, they'd drop their packs to the ground and drape their little bodies over them, trying to rest and stretch sore shoulders, backs, hips, and legs. We'd gaze up the dramatic cliff faces, sometimes not even able to see the sky due to the canyon narrowing above our heads. We talked about the geologic processes that formed such an impressive canyon. We marveled at huge boulders and trees lodged between the canyon walls, both amazed and terrified by the thought of the powerful floods that deposited such massive objects 50-plus feet above our heads. Most miles we sang songs, played hiking games, told stories, and appreciated out loud the ruggedness and beauty all around. We'd occasionally walk in silence, but it never lasted long, usually broken by Story spotting a large boulder and asking hopefully, "Is that the rock jam?!" She knew the rock jam was our final obstacle before the confluence of Buckskin and the Paria River, our destination for the day. As much as we talk about enjoying the journey, six-year-olds are understandably pretty concerned with the destination—particularly with how much longer until we get there.

With nightfall fast approaching, I was growing increasingly concerned with the destination myself. We did reach the rock jam before dark, but this obstacle changes some with each flood, and current conditions were trickier than we were hoping. Kids always add an extra layer of trickiness to any canyon obstacle, and there was no straightforward rappel down this time. The never-ending pool section had majorly slowed us down, and now we were facing the decision of descending the drop in the dark or backtracking the other direction to a section of slightly higher ground and camping there for the night. I detested both options. At first, I insisted we keep going because you just absolutely do not, under any circumstances, ever camp in a narrow canyon. Brandon, a much more levelheaded risk assessor than me, talked out the pros and cons of each option. Long story short, we ended up camping in the canyon, as hesitant as I am to even share that because it just goes against everything I know about backcountry canyon safety; but under the current circumstances I was forced to acknowledge our options were far from black and white.

The kids were exhausted and needed sleep, the bats were starting to spook Vi and Story, the likelihood of someone getting injured increases when repelling and hiking in the dark (despite great headlamps, an already dark canyon after the sun goes down is really freaking dark), we had no way of knowing if we'd run into more pools after the rock jam and before the confluence (turned out, as we learned the next morning, we would, and that would have been dangerous in the dark with already cold temperatures dropping even lower). We determined the safest and smartest thing, or I guess it was the next safest and smartest thing because we'd moved too slow to stick to the initial safest and smartest plan, was to stop and camp where we were currently, or at least relatively, safe. Brandon remembered passing a slightly higher, flat and sandy section where we could fit the tent. We packed up the rope, put packs back on, and started retracing our steps. My head filled with worst-case scenarios.

For about as long as I can remember, I've had this habit of reading, rather obsessively, everything I can about the type of disasters I hope to avoid. In planning a Glacier National Park trip, I read countless stories of grizzly bear attacks, trying to connect some dots, make any sense of when/if you should play dead or fight back. Apparently bear bells aren't effective (haha, I'd been carrying and annoying my brother-in-law with those for years), bear spray is effective, but only if you spray it with solid accuracy into the bear's face and at a crazy close distance (sounds like a reasonable ask of anyone face-to-face with a grizzly—not). I think I ultimately concluded, after reading one study that outlined a correlation between bear attacks and bears suffering from severe tooth decay, I was left to just hope we only run into bears with good dental hygiene whose teeth aren't making them grouchy and aggressive.

Another example, in an attempt to try and like the ocean more than I actually do (I'm a major land lover), I had a phase of researching shark attacks. On that front, I finally decided that despite the incredibly low risk of me ever encountering an aggressive or confused shark, my fear of the ocean outweighs my love of it, so most days I simply embrace my place on the beach. Jude always gives me a hard time over this. One Southern California trip when he was young and ecstatic to play in the ocean, he asked me, "Are you sure you don't want to get all the way in, Mom? If I didn't get in the ocean today, I'd regret it for the rest of my life!" Gotta love him trying to spare me future regret.

My love of desert adventures and slot canyons, however, has always motivated any and every effort it takes to move myself and especially my kids safely through them. So, naturally, I've gone down plenty of desert disaster and survival story rabbit holes, particularly with flash floods. I know flash foods can surprise you from distant thunder storms you didn't even know were happening, canyons can fill with water hours after a storm has passed, and you often have mere seconds warning to move to higher ground before a wall of water and debris is racing toward you.

In Utah, we aren't hurting for accounts of flash floods; I've read and reread too many. The most salient and sad as I write this now is one that hadn't even happened at the time we were crossing Buckskin. It would be almost a year later when two young kids were caught and killed in a different canyon in south central Utah. I still get sick to my stomach thinking of that family and take a moment to send those parents love and peace at the entrance of every canyon I've explored since.

Mountains, desert canyons, the wild backcountry—places I feel so happy and at home; as much as I love them, I am also scared of them. It's a healthy fear, an important balance. We had checked and rechecked the forecast of Buckskin and the entire surrounding area countless times while preparing for this adventure and compiling trip beta. I had consumed all available weather information and was left with plenty of reasons to trust the canyon wouldn't fill with water anytime soon. I knew camping before the confluence was the wisest choice given our circumstances, and while I wasn't able to sleep a wink that night—I stayed wide awake listening for rumblings of distant thunder or goats falling from the rim, wanting to get my family the eff out of that canyon—I also wondered at Brandon and my ability to problem solve without panicking or arguing. How'd we just do that? I knew this decision (of where to stop and camp for the night) would have escalated into a big fight when we were married.

Over the years I've continued marveling at this phenomenon— Brandon and I becoming better problem solvers, better communicators, better teammates post-divorce. I think it has a lot to do with canceling and resetting all agreements and expectations. With divorce comes so much shattering, so much breaking down, so much change. Step four in the Conscious Uncoupling program is Become a Love Alchemist (Thomas 2016). To be honest, I thought this was a silly, fluffy, nonsense step when I first read the book in the earliest stages of my divorce. But I get it now. Even after the most painful of undoings, it is possible to rebuild something beautiful. Our successful Buckskin adventure felt like such a huge payoff in this process. I couldn't have been prouder of or happier with our healing family.

Pictures

Even divorce might be seen as one kind of fulfillment of love. Love asks many things of us, including actions that seem to be utterly counter to feelings of attachment and loyalty. (Moore quoted in Thomas 2016, 27)

Hard to believe it's been nearly two years since Brandon and I felt (and desperately hoped) divorce was the right thing. Yesterday we spent a beautiful Christmas together—not the same family, but definitely not broken—more like a healthy, happy evolving one. Those moments of clarity, recognizing the really hard thing was the right thing still overwhelms me with feelings of both sadness and gratitude. Figured today was a good day to share something both difficult and beautiful.

Post-divorce family pictures are HARD for me. The day Brandon and kids were taking their pictures I ran 40ish miles from North Ogden Divide to Mantua and back…And I know by now there's no running those monsters out of my chest, but it quiets them and gives me better perspective. And I absolutely love the pictures kids and I took with my family over Thanksgiving…I think they just serve as reminders that this process, like most things that require change and growth, is bittersweet. Whatever the future holds, I trust Brandon and I will hold space for each other as dear friends and co-parents.

I love our unconventional family so dang much. And if I would have been on top of it enough to send unconventional family holiday cards this year, they would have included a few of these pictures. Sending lots of light and love! (@megbcampbell December 26, 2019)

We humans love our pictures. Throughout all of human history, we've been compelled to document our experience on this planet with pictures. From petroglyphs to Chatbooks, our documenting has evolved with us. We're enthralled with photo albums full of pictures of relatives long since passed, our own baby photos, or those of our friends. Finding a picture of your friend as a baby in a bathtub will elicit a giggle from any middle schooler.

Kids today can't even fathom the patience we had to exercise growing up with film cameras—having to actually be more thoughtful with our picture taking because we didn't have unlimited takes, then waiting until the end of the roll to turn it in for development, waiting longer still for the film to be processed and pictures printed. Now we examine each photo mere seconds after it's taken. Talk about fewer and fewer opportunities to practice delayed gratification. (Though, if you're reading this and working on a gracious divorce, that's the ultimate practice of delaying gratification!)

Family pictures—these were rough. I'm not totally sure why either. I'm not all that sentimental of a person. I think lots of "sentimentalism" is simply scarcity with a softer name. My kids keep all kinds of crap stuffed in corners of closets, buried in nightstand drawers, shoved in deep pockets and surviving multiple laundry cycles but not necessarily because they're sentimental. I think it's because of that primitive "not enough" mentality that takes a few decades to challenge or condition out. We all know that temptation to convince ourselves, *I'll need or use it someday!* (Or maybe we don't even believe that, we just really can't stand the idea of someone else having it instead.) On de-junking days I'll chant, "Don't be a hoarder, get your crap in order" when the kids try to convince me they *need* a single jack to a set long since lost or half a deck of tattered playing cards or, occasionally, garbage. Anyone else's kids literally argue over garbage?!

I think family pictures were especially hard because I had a solid collection of lovely, past family pictures. Pre-divorce, I would stare at these pictures and shame myself for contemplating ending my marriage. *Look at this beautiful family, look how perfect. What kind of mom wants to break this up?* Our little family did look dang good in photos, on paper, in theory. For years we clung to that blissful idea while denying daily evidence to the contrary, trying to convince ourselves it was enough, should be enough. Yes, in hindsight I understand the dangers of those particular shoulds, but that doesn't invalidate how hard it was at the time to not constantly question if this major course deviation was the right thing for our family. Family pictures set off those second-guessing alarms loud and strong.

For you it may not be family pictures, maybe it's Taco Tuesday and missing your former spouse who always seasoned the meat perfectly, maybe it's not being there to hug your kids before bed three nights out of the week, maybe it's the first few times you check the box "single" or "divorced" on a form at the doctor's office. (I find those boxes confusing, by the way—it's not like those options are mutually exclusive—should I check both?) I don't have any great advice here, other than to not fight these consequences of divorce or try to bury the hurt they induce. We hurt because we tried for something, we loved someone, we experienced loss; dwelling on any perceived injustice behind the hurt will leave you stuck. Acknowledging it, feeling it, working to understand your role in it while continuing onward is more productive. It's not easy, but I have yet to hear it claimed that healing is.

> That place of true healing is a fierce place. It's a giant place. It's a place of monstrous beauty and endless dark and glimmering light. And you have to work really, really, really hard to get there, but you can do it. (Strayed 2015, 56)

PART 5

2020

Star Stuff

I feel like a part of my soul has loved you since the beginning of everything. Maybe we're from the *same* star. (Allen 2010)

It was Valentine's Day 12 years ago I found out I was pregnant with Jude…I was instantly and madly in love. I was also panicking at the thought of all the Diet Coke and unpasteurized cheese I'd ingested the weeks before. So crazy to remember a time before knowing and loving these three.

This last week Violet helped Story paint her volcano Valentine box, Jude took Story to the "walking report card" portion of first grade parent-teacher conferences, they've helped each other with lots of reading, homework and hobbies…Plus they put up with my getting out paper Santa plates instead of finding our Valentine dishes for fondue tonight.

I'm lucky to be their mom…Love them bigger than the universe. (@megbcampbell February 14, 2020)

During the existential crisis of my early thirties, I had a really difficult time curbing my curiosity. That's not a bad thing—wanting to keep exploring, learning, re-evaluating. At a time when so many previously held beliefs were being completely debunked, I couldn't stop wondering, *What else am I wrong about?* and it was rabbit hole after rabbit hole after rabbit hole. I read texts like *On Being Wrong* by Kathryn Shultz (2011), Richard Dawkins's *The God Delusion* (2006), *Astrophysics for People in a Hurry* by Neil deGrasse Tyson (2017), and Carl Sagan's *Pale Blue Dot* (1994). That one became an all-time favorite reminder of how both big and small we are.

So much work went into me finally determining how very little I know. From faith and identity crises to divorce, that was an unsettling deconstruction! I now, however, take comfort in the idea of all there is yet to be discovered and am fascinated by all there is yet to be understood. I certainly prefer this surrender and curiosity over trying to blindly believe anything. I don't have answers for myself or my kids about how exactly we came to be or what happens after we die. We discuss what is known—like what Carl Sagan explained while narrating the PBS series *Cosmos: A Personal Voyage* (Malone 1980), that we are literally made of star stuff: "The nitrogen in our DNA, the calcium in our teeth, the iron in our blood, the carbon in our apple pies were made in the interiors of collapsing stars. We are made of star stuff."

Most assume that Emery Allen "from the same star" quote above is referencing a lover. And maybe it is, likely even that's the case; my teenage-soulmate-believing self would have romanticized the crap out of that idea. But coming across it as a parent, of course it's about my kids. My soul has loved them since the beginning of everything—my pure and huge love for them makes more sense to me than any and everything else I have studied, researched, worked to understand— it's my most evident truth. Coming from the same star is my favorite explanation of that core knowing and core loving them.

Recalling this random account of Valentine's Day hecticness, I remember Story's unique volcano valentine's box she had to waddle to carry to and from school, so proud of the creation Vi and her had worked together on. I remember Jude genuinely complimenting Story on how well she was doing in first grade and how hard she works after joining her on that walking report card (where hands-on tasks were set up for students to demonstrate learning for parents, or occasionally an

11-year-old brother when Mom was hosting her own parent-teacher conferences down the hall).

I remember feeling a pang of guilt that evening that I hadn't even gotten out our box of Valentine's Day decorations, which meant I also hadn't gotten out our fun Valentine's Day dishes—heart-shaped plates with cutesy creatures making clever comments, like the owl reminding you, *Owl always love you!* Or the kitty who thinks you're a *Purrfect Valentine!* I remember standing in my pantry, trying to shut down some critical self-talk, reaching for the Santa paper plates left over from Christmas and resolving to stay present for our fruit and fondue. And it was lovely. Brandon joined us and I can still visualize all their candlelit smiling faces, their stories, their laughter. Despite how busy and chaotic my life felt some days, these windows of real and quality time together was worth everything I occasionally worried divorce cost me.

New Memories

With my birthday falling on Easter this year, I got to celebrate early with new shoes and a run. I ran from Beus to North Ogden Divide, with each kid joining me for a section—Story ran one mile, Violet ran three and Jude ran five—and when I say run, like actual trail running. They absolutely amazed me and were the best trail buddies ever!!

This sweet gift was more profound than even I guessed when we started planning it. I spent a lot of heart heavy miles on this section of the Bonneville Shoreline Trail in the past. Even with over a couple years between those painful times and now, I wasn't sure I'd ever totally disassociate it from the hurt. This gift was so much more than a run—it was new memories, new associations. On the same trail I used to run and cry and worry endlessly about my family and how we'd all survive a divorce; now I was running and talking and laughing with my beautiful kids. And Brandon met me at four different trailheads to exchange them and shuttle me back to my car. Thankfully the goal shifted from simply surviving a divorce to thriving as an unconventional family, and there's no one else I'd rather be co-parenting these amazing humans with.

Despite not being in as good of shape this year, I can't remember ever feeling more light and happy on a run. I told the kids this may become an annual thing; just can't imagine topping this birthday. Thank you, Brandon, Jude, Vi and Story…Love you all so big. (@megbcampbell April 12, 2020)

The Bonneville Shoreline Trail (BST) is a long trail system, roughly following the shoreline of the ancient Lake Bonneville that used to cover most of northwestern Utah, even stretching into present-day Idaho and Nevada at its largest. The BST runs north to south along the foothills of the Wasatch Mountains, weaving in and out of various canyons for over 100 miles. There are a few sections along the east bench of Ogden, Utah, that I've spent a great deal of time on over the years. This particular BST section I ran on my birthday was full of emotionally charged memories and associations. One tree in particular—I've run under its beautiful golden leaves in the fall and bare gray branches in the winter, ducked under its thick green leaves in the spring and early summer. Year after year after year I marvel at its resilience, its stable presence, its ability to adapt to the changing of seasons. More than once I've found Fleetwood Mac's "Landslide" lyrics filling my head upon passing under it.

Other landmarks reminded me of tired runs after sleepless nights, some climbs elicited memories of hard conversations with Brandon, one corner always reminds me of the time I was so lost in thought and worry that I ran down the wrong trail straight into a homeless camp. I've had a few encounters with transient individuals who I know camp along various sections of the BST, ranging from harmless (commenting on the beautiful weather and wishing me a nice run) to uncomfortable (asking me where I parked, where I'm headed, if I ever get separated from my dog Molly, or if she's known to be aggressive). Panic set in as I looked around, my headlamp illuminating piles of trash the same moment the smell reached my nose. I avoided primitive firepits and tarps draped over tree branches as I retraced my steps as quickly and quietly as I could, scolding myself for being so distracted and reckless. (I'm not implying homeless individuals are opportunistic and would harm me for passing by. Putting myself in a situation where I lose track of where I am and where I'm going alone in the still-dark hours of the early morning is simply unwise.)

Perhaps needless to say, I developed an interesting relationship with the BST. I'd go there in so much pain, but usually leave in slightly less, creating all sorts of confusing and contradictory feelings that I was never clear where or how to attribute. This birthday run was a reset I didn't know I needed. I'd passively resigned to that "complicated" relationship—but why? Now when something or someone or someplace elicits a painful or confusing divorce-related memory, instead of trying to ignore or explain it away as inevitable, I acknowledge it, explore it, try to understand it, but also give myself permission to reset it. We don't have to live hostage to past memories and associations. Of course, certain things may always pain us to recall, but don't give those things so much power that they continually rob how wonderful the present could be. I'm so grateful my family gifted me this run, and also grateful I accepted.

Space to Be

> If you have young children, give them help, guidance, and protection to the best of your ability, but even more important, give them space—space to be. They come into this world through you, but they are not 'yours.' The belief 'I know what's best for you' may be true when they are very young, but the older they get, the less true it becomes. The more expectations you have of how their life should unfold, the more you are in your mind instead of being present for them. (Tolle 2005, 101)

When I first read these words in *A New Earth*, I knew it was something important I needed to understand better...How extraordinary and humbling I get to know and love these incredible humans as their mom. They are patient and kind

WITH GRACE AND GRATITUDE

and let me try to fix things when I mess up. I love you, Jude, Violet, and Story!! (@megbcampbell May 10, 2020)

I shared this on Mother's Day, my third Mother's Day as an unmarried mom, and during a time I was working to learn more and challenge some past ideas about what my role of "Mom" entailed. This idea of *space to be* really struck me. I couldn't remember feeling any of my own space to be for many years. I think it was leaving a church, choosing to divorce, deviating from those obvious paths that gave me even an understanding of *space to be*. Brandon agrees divorce, including much that led up to and followed, was the catalyst for his space to be as well.

Finally refusing to live by many of my prescribed shoulds allowed me to also table any such shoulds I might have otherwise had or developed for my own kids. That right there is among the biggest gifts of my personal divorce journey. It's so wonderfully simple. I get to be present and enjoy my front-row seat to raising kids with space to be, empowered to follow their cores, shape their best lives, and hopefully always trust in my unconditional love. That's the dream.

I text Brandon while reflecting on this section, commenting I felt divorce made us better parents, how I thought we were doing a good job both loving our kids really big and also giving them this space to be, thanking him for being such a good dad, saying I was proud of us. His response: "I totally agree. I think it started with leaving the church…that process really led to exploring what other standards we were living by that we didn't actually like or agree with. I think that largely contributed to our divorce, which led to lots of other practices and ways of living that ultimately make us and the kids happier and more free."

Yep, that. Pursue what feels aligned with your core and provides you and those you love all *space to be*.

Bittersweet

I took down the last wedding photo today. Two years and three months after our divorce was final. Exploring the reasons behind this. The photo was in a difficult to reach and out of the way spot on the wall, I also didn't want our kids to be hurt or sad at pictures of their parents together just disappearing overnight. Still, lots of time (and repression) between overnight and over two years.

A friend recently mentioned she was grieving the loss of her marriage. I was speechless. Watching her move forward with divorce a couple of years after me, I could mostly empathize with what she was going through, but I couldn't remember this particular phase, couldn't remember grieving the loss of my marriage. How is that possible? I was devastated over losing the traditional family I'd known. I specifically remember grieving the loss of future memories never to be made together (mostly with regard to our kids and their life milestones that wouldn't see their married parents in attendance). I think I was so overwhelmed and terrified over what the divorce meant for our family and kids' futures, I didn't consciously grieve the enormous loss of Brandon and me as a couple, and taking down this last reminder that there was a time we completely chose one another and committed to building a life together— it kinda punched me in the throat.

I'm feeling the weight of this loss today, years later and heavier than ever. I'm both so sorry and so grateful. I know regret rather intimately by 37 years old, and Brandon's been around for my bigger screw-ups...but I look at our incredible kids and wouldn't do a thing differently, couldn't risk not ending up exactly where we all are right now. Bittersweet. (Journal entry from June 17, 2020)

I don't think I'm alone in skipping this step, unfortunately. With all the logistics of how to get divorced, especially if kids are involved, we lose sight of the who. Who we are divorcing gets too easily overwhelmed by the worry over how to break up a family unit, the anxiety over dividing resources, the concern of how to adequately support kids through all of it, the very personal terror that accompanies all this unraveling. When it comes down to the most basic process of two individuals uncoupling, chances are other, less primary relationships were given space for more sadness and grief at their close than is typically granted an ending marriage. This is exacerbated when anyone becomes more concerned with "winning" than treating their former partner civilly; spouses begin dehumanizing each other, deeply damaging the prospect of getting to one day fully mourn the loss.

Be gentle with yourself if/when this immense grief surprises you. Breathe and lean into it, notice where you feel it in your body, acknowledge it, understand you are hurting and grieving because you were part of something both beautiful and hard that ran its course and was bravely released. Send your former partner love—not the same you once felt romantically for them—but the wise and pure kind born of risk, hurt, growth, and hope.

A Wild Heart

> The mark of a wild heart is living out the paradox of love in our lives. It's the ability to be tough and tender, excited and scared, brave and afraid...all in the same moment. It's showing up in our vulnerability and our courage, being both fierce and kind.
>
> Always straddling the tension and trying not to tap out. Forever convincing ourselves that we can hold so many contradictory pieces and feelings. Not only are tension and contradictory pieces OK and normal—they're the magic sauce.
>
> Carl Jung called the paradox one of our most valued spiritual possessions and a great witness to the truth. He wrote, 'Only the paradox comes anywhere near to comprehending the fullness of life.'
>
> Sometimes beautiful. Sometimes terrible. Always deeply human. (Brown 2020)

Holding both is hard. That tension is hard. Not tapping out is hard. Deeply human is hard and marvelous.

"I'm sorry you had to make multiple copies of everything and do separate conferences for us. Our divorce still feels pretty fresh; Jeni's mom and I are doing our best, but not to the point of sharing a parent-teacher conference appointment yet."

It's always a privilege when anyone shares some of their pain, articulates that tension, and is deeply human with you. There was zero need or reason for this father to apologize—he showed up for his kindergarten daughter's parent-teacher conference, just as her mom had hours earlier. They both expressed genuine interest in prioritizing their child's well-being, which they were doing wonderfully. After over a decade in early childhood education, I can spot an emotionally thriving kindergartener. Neither parent spoke negatively of the other, even though both were hurting, trying to hold so much, not tapping out.

Divorce doesn't need to unfold or look a certain way. These co-parents needn't feel pressure to attend a parent-teacher conference together if they're not comfortable with that; they simply need to keep prioritizing their kids' health and sense of safety. Clearly, their daughter felt free to love both parents really big—she'd come to class with stories about what she did with her dad over the weekend or a perler bead creation she made with her Mom. I overheard her explain to classmates that she has two homes (because her parents are divorced) with an ease I'm convinced comes from knowing she belongs, she is loved, she is safe in both. Do whatever it takes to co-parent in a manner that allows your kids to feel and trust that, then don't fret over other aspects you worry "should" look different.

It's all too easy for parents to torture themselves over not being able to protect kids from potentially embarrassing or difficult circumstances, then feel the need to apologize to outsiders over perceived or imagined parental missteps. In these instances, perhaps we are overthinking. When you are making necessary decisions from a place of prioritizing your kids' overall health to the greatest extent possible within your control, also trust that kids are incredibly resilient, and anyone worth including in your circle will celebrate and support your efforts and your deep humanness.

Messy and Beautiful and All Over the Place

Sometimes, even over two and a half years post-divorce, I still find myself suffocating from guilt over past choices and worry over future trajectories.

Mid-Covid pandemic, but life in Utah is back to a new and somehow busier normal. I am in my final semester of graduate school, working as a graduate teaching assistant 20 hours a week for a past professor (figured I better start thinking about how I'm going to pay off all my student loans), and teaching full time (though my responsibilities have increased significantly in trying to meet the learning needs of both my in-person and online students).

My own kids' schedules are crazier than ever, and I simply can't keep up. Not only is this level of crazy-busy not sustainable, it's also not what I want. I miss my kids. I miss being home when they get home from school, I miss tucking them in nights I'm at class, I miss being around more for the big and little things, for all of it.

This window of my kids being young and home and caring if I'm around or not is closing quick. I know I can't slow down or change that, but feeling powerless to change my circumstances and do more, unable to be more present in this window is killing me.

You should have stayed married, you could be home...You wouldn't be so poor and stressed about money all the time, you wouldn't be drowning in debt...It was good enough...Divorce was dumb, it was selfish, look at all it's cost your family...Look at all you've lost...What were you thinking?

I know, I know this head space is unhealthy and unhelpful. I can hear and feel the scarcity. I should be challenging it. I can rationally address and counter all of those points. I understand the married life I'm missing tonight didn't exist years ago and wouldn't exist now if we'd somehow managed to just stick it out. It's a beautiful idea of a memory I'll conjure occasionally to fuel the mom guilt, but I honestly can't guess at the kind of people Brandon and I would be today had we stayed unhappily married. So tonight, in trying to halt my unproductive spiraling through all the things I could or should have done differently three years ago, I'm trying to breathe through-the-through, and write it out. (Journal entry from September 1, 2020)

You will work through things you thought were behind you over and over and over again. That doesn't mean you're doing something wrong. Healing isn't a linear process. Healing is messy and beautiful and all over the place. Some days you'll feel you're rocking it, other days you'll feel you're failing miserably; this doesn't suggest you've made no progress.

One Saturday morning, Jude (age 13 at the time) had headed downstairs to pick up his room. His easy-going, fun-is-the-best nature lends itself to never caring too much about the typically messy state of his room. On any given day I'm likely to find the floor cluttered with anything from hoodies to books to guitars to random charging chords and climbing gear. This particular morning warranted a pickup because he'd let his four-year-old cousin dump boxes of his old Legos out a few days before, and he was finally tiring of stepping on them. I went down about an hour later, curious if he was almost ready to head to the climbing gym (like we'd discussed doing that afternoon) and was shocked to find how very little he'd picked up. Despite being familiar with his tendency to get sidetracked mid-chore—like en route to replace a book on the bookshelf, he'll sit down and start reading it instead, or he'll notice his guitar in the middle of putting away laundry and take a break to play a few songs—this morning's progress appeared painfully slow, even for Jude.

"Have you done anything? Seriously, it looks like you've made zero progress," I exclaimed.

Jude, calm and smiling at my outburst, replied, "I don't think you understand the definition of progress. Progress doesn't mean anything needs to be observable right away, it just means you've done a little. You're closer than you were when you started."

Even if this is a rather lame excuse for slow room-cleaning progress, and Jude wasn't trying to be all philosophical so much as distract me with some witty reasoning, it still struck me as rather profound.

While progress and healing neither will nor need to look a certain way, something that remains consistent throughout is the importance of obtaining help and support when you need it. Just like I knew I needed Kate (my conscious uncoupling coach) to get through my divorce, I once again needed an oxygen mask; I needed some help to keep showing up for myself and my kids, and in a manner I could look back on and not only live with, but be proud of.

It started with me opening up to Shera, telling her how overwhelmed I'd been feeling. And I don't use the adjective "overwhelmed" here lightly; my nervous system was dysregulated and majorly struggling. Something needed to give or change. I couldn't adequately keep up with the demands of my life. I didn't have enough time, energy, or money…I confided how all these concerns lead to feelings of intense guilt and shame and questioning if the kids wouldn't be better off had Brandon and I stayed married. Being single was feeling super scary.

It was in this exchange I also shared how I was absolutely dreading my next period. If I was feeling overwhelmed generally, the week before and of my period were a nightmare. I felt out of control, unable to curb the flooding of strong and difficult emotions, I could and would cry often and easily. It was getting ridiculous. On top of the mental and emotional havoc my period was increasingly wreaking, the physical pelvic floor and right leg pain it triggered was starting to interfere with my day-to-day responsibilities. I don't know all the physiology behind it, but however my body carried both my girls while pregnant compromised major vein systems on the right side of my lower body. Two weeks of every month, those damaged veins, from my uterus down to my right ankle, would painfully throb and ache nearly nonstop, despite some pricey waist-high support hose, regular elevation of my leg, and excessive ibuprofen. Shera listened to and loved me, then she suggested I both make an appointment with my gynecologist and seek specialized support for working moms. Essentially, she oh so gently encouraged me to stop whining and start problem-solving.

The gyno appointment was easy. Not sure why I'd put this off so long. I didn't want to entertain the possibility of major surgery yet (that had been presented as an option years ago). I didn't think I wanted to get back on birth control pills either (thought those hormones would make me somehow more "crazy"). Mostly, I didn't want to admit or talk about how bad I was struggling. But I definitely should have made this happen earlier. My doctor is fantastic, and over the next couple of years, we dialed in a solution. I had my veins treated, I no longer have a traditional period, I don't experience the extreme emotional waves I used to every month, and the only physical symptom remaining is pretty painless blood occasionally pooling in my right leg. I wouldn't even know it was that time of the month except someone will usually ask about the "bruise" on my calf. I used to try and tell myself, *It's only once a month, suck it up*. But once a month was really two weeks a month, and two weeks a month is half the month, which turns into half a year, which turns into half the rest of my life! Shera helped remind me I am worth the help and support I was single-handedly withholding. Next step was calling Katy Blommer.

Balance and Values

I'd met Katy a couple of times before, she's a good friend of Shera's, a successful executive at a large financial institution, also founder of Women's Best Life University and creator of The Working Mom Happiness Method. I was lucky to connect with Katy when she was getting ready to launch the first group session of her Working Mom Happiness Method program, "a 10-week program designed to help working moms create balance, maintain healthy habits, and achieve their career and personal goals" (Blommer 2020). After a consultation call consisting of me sharing a little about my current situation and concerns, and Katy then sharing how the program could benefit me, I enrolled. This was another big financial commitment for me; the argument could have certainly been made that I couldn't afford this. Katy customized a monthly payment plan I could manage because, once again, I also couldn't afford to not obtain the help. I majorly needed support with balance in general, time management, challenging mom guilt, finding time to still pursue personal goals, creating a fulfilling life within the existing parameters I'd chosen/created—and this program was an amazing fit.

Where to start trying to articulate all I learned in this program?! I suppose lots of it was stuff I knew on some level—concepts and ideas I'd heard and claimed to believe—but actually and finally better understanding and putting so much into practice was life-changing. As I worked through the program, I began internalizing some important and powerful themes:

- I have innate value and worth, not dependent on what I can do for others, not contingent on anything I do or don't accomplish.

- I am responsible for my own life and happiness—others may enhance it, but it cannot be outsourced.

- Setting and honoring boundaries, both with myself and with others, is key to protecting my time and energy.

- I am most happy, present, and alive when I spend my time in line with my core values.

These may seem simple and obvious, but they're also easy to overlook or stop honoring when resources (time, energy, money) are stressed. We get busy, easily distracted, tempted to embrace others' shoulds instead of our own; the various demands of daily life often leave us spread so thin, we start operating on auto-pilot and forget the point: to live, to be, to love.

In order to spend our time in line with our values, we first must get really clear on what we actually and truly value. This assignment (to think about and record our personal values) in and of itself was eye-opening: various values instilled since childhood remained, some I was in the middle of challenging, others gone altogether. While I knew I'd adopted some new values in recent years, it wasn't until this exercise I worked to prioritize them. Katy provided a values outline, and the only thing she instructed was that we list ourselves first.

I was really uncomfortable with that directive. Before I even moved forward with this step in the program, I got on the phone with her to make my case for listing my kids first instead. *They are my entire world, the depth of my love for and value of them is immeasurable, it feels objectively inaccurate to not list them first!* Katy listened and gently explained that addressing this confliction is the point of the whole program.

The structure and system we're born into often sets us up to lose ourselves in pursuit of various overarching values and shoulds we inherit, with no understanding of how to evaluate or determine if we actually embrace them. Katy wisely used my powerful love and concern for my kids to illustrate the importance of valuing myself first and foremost.

"Would you ever want Jude, Violet, or Story to grow up and value something or someone else more than themselves? What do you want them to understand and believe about who is accountable for them, for their lives, their happiness? I understand it's difficult to claim you value yourself above anything and everyone else. That is the result of both years of conditioning and, of course, the huge love you do feel for your kids. But your kids deserve a mom and a role model who values herself, her health, her life. Where will they learn to value themselves and pursue their best lives if they don't see their parents model it? I promise you will be a better mom and have even stronger relationships with them as you start living in line with valuing yourself most. It feels uncomfortable, even dishonest right now, still I challenge you to list yourself first, and work on honoring that all-important value."

I reluctantly agreed, and here's what I came up with by the end of our values module:

1. Myself

    • Kind, present, authentic

- Choosing courage over comfort, being vulnerable
- Mountains, desert, adventure
- Show up, love full throttle, fix it after you fuck up (hat tip to Cheryl Strayed)
- Keep learning always
- Work hard, play hard, strong boundaries (balance of preparedness and spontaneity), spread goodwill

2. My Family

- Being present and connected most with Jude, Violet, and Story
- Continuing to build a healthy friendship and co-parenting relationship with Brandon
- Raising kind, confident, and happy kids who feel comfortable and brave enough to follow their own passions in life
- Loving my kids exactly as they are and not trying to turn them into something/someone else—act in accordance with my goal that they will always feel unconditionally loved and accepted
- Helping my kids develop positive self-concepts and gain a genuine belief in their own inherent value and worth

3. Family Adventures: big and small (from southern Utah, to Banff, Canada, to Costa Rica)

4. Bucket List Runs (Rim-to-Rim-to-Rim, Uinta Highline, Colorado Fourteeners)

5. Work and Learning

- Instill in my kids a value of education and knowledge, empower them to ask questions
- Support my kids in pursuing learning and hobbies they love

- Be a positive influence in the lives of students I teach/work with

6. Friends and Extended Family

    • Invest in relationships that feel good/warm/safe

7. A home the kids and I feel comfortable and safe in

    • Remain in our family home (until kids graduate)

8. Earning enough money to support myself and the kids

    • Pay for meaningful activities/experiences

    • Save for kids' college

    • Travel as a family

9. Coffee

I wasn't exactly on board with this outline at the time, but looking back I can see myself trying to embrace Katy's challenge of valuing myself first while still honoring certain things that were, are, and will always be true. (My kids and coffee will forever make the values list!)

I was grateful for this opportunity to put my core values down in writing. As I progressed through the course, learning about and working on boundaries, goal setting, relationships and how I show up in them, time management and protecting my energy...I recognized how these constructs are connected and realized I actually have a great deal of power over deciding how to spend my minutes, hours, and days in line with what I value most. Throughout the course of the program, I experienced wins ranging from drinking more water, making dinner four times a week (that was huge for me!), and not forgetting garbage day, to bigger ones like completing grad school and passing my school counselor licensure exam, registering and more consistently training for ultramarathons, growing more connected to my kids, feeling less overwhelmed and more empowered to simply experience this one life.

Another favorite and powerful exercise from the course was drafting affirmation and goal statements, all stated in the affirmative. At one point I wrote, "I can quiet my mind, I can be still." In the word program I was typing in, it underlined "can" and asked, "*Do you mean can't?*" Ha! Even this program knew better and was encouraging me with that blue squiggly underline to revise it to more accurately read, "I can't quiet my mind…" which has been the case most of my life. Comparisons to "monkey mind" or "Squirrel!" problems are all too relatable. I used to dismiss mindfulness and meditation as simply not for me, my mind doesn't work that way.

While I'm still far from stellar at being still, I started meditating more consistently through my divorce, more frequently still through this program, and it *is* something that can be learned, a skill that can be cultivated, a practice that has enhanced my overall health and happiness. I was the skeptic of skeptics when it came to anything remotely this hippy-woo-woo-ey, but now am passionate about carving out time daily to check in, reflect and be still. There are extensive resources and options available to support beginning a meditation practice. Start with peaceful music, breathing exercises, a guided meditation—there's dozens of apps—just start somewhere. One of the first guided meditation courses I participated in was Sarah Blondin's Coming Home to Yourself (2018). For less than 15 minutes a day, over the course of 10 days, I was encouraged to explore my inner world and gently guided toward meeting my empowered self. (I participated in the entirety of this course twice, appreciating both the wisdom and direction it provided while I was developing this new skill of being still.) Learning to go inward, to find and meet yourself outside of the hustle and away from the distracting background noise, is magical.

Big Boobs and Straight Teeth

I was sitting in my ophthalmologist's office outlining my dilemma of whether I should commit to a LASIK procedure or not. I'd had very poor eyesight for about as long as I could remember. I started wearing glasses in my early elementary years. By fifth grade I was in contact lenses, and I loved my contacts. It was incredible—a thin, flexible circle of plastic could correct my horrible vision. Upon first learning about evolution, Darwin and survival of the fittest, I marveled at how lucky I was to be born after we'd outsmarted some natural selection processes. I was legally blind without corrective lenses and would have likely not survived to adulthood with my eyesight had I been born just a few hundred years earlier. Wild!

I rationalized that I was so used to my contacts and had no complaints; if I was going to invest in an elective procedure, I would probably choose breast augmentation or orthodontic work before LASIK. I'm friends with this eye doctor and his family, so he was somewhat familiar with my interests and values. I'm paraphrasing here, I know he was much more professional and tactful with the delivery, but he said something to the effect that the result of those investments—i.e., big boobs and straight teeth—wouldn't save my life if I were on top of a technical mountain and lost a contact lens. I chuckled, then also got wondering why I thought I valued or wanted big boobs or straighter teeth to begin with. (Hell, I had four, yes four, rounds of braces in my middle school through college years. I'm sure my still-slightly-crooked teeth have something to do with poor retainer-wearing habits. Sorry, Mom and Dad. Dang, that's frustrating now that Brandon and I are paying for our own kids' orthodontic work!)

I didn't actually care about big boobs or straighter teeth all that much for myself, but I was motivated to escape the scarcity and stress I felt after divorce at the possibility of no one being attracted to or wanting me again. (I don't mean to sound critical of such elective procedures; I support anyone pursuing these things as an act of self-interest and care. At the time, I was simply entertaining them for the wrong reasons.)

My ophthalmologist was correct, LASIK was most in line with my values. I still took a few months deliberating, but ultimately moved forward with LASIK, and I couldn't be more thrilled with my now-near-perfect vision. It was mind-blowing—to be able to see in the middle of the night and first thing in the morning, to not have to deal with contacts on camping or backpacking trips, never having to stop on the side of a ski run because wind blew a contact off the center of my eye, never worrying about losing or tearing a contact mid-adventure. My only regret is not getting LASIK sooner!

Over the past couple of years I've noticed such an increase in overall peace. Even when days are jam-packed, we're racing from one activity to the next, there's a to-do list of chores a mile long...I feel more balanced, more present, more in control, overall more comfortable and content in my own skin—crooked teeth, small boobs and all! Choosing to value myself first feels more natural now, and living in line with core values more clear.

PART 6

2021

The Universe (Catching)

Good morning fellow graduates, families and friends...

My name is Meg Campbell, and I'm thrilled to be here today, graduating with my master of education in psychology. I'm fortunate to know some of your stories, and can only guess at others in this room, but would imagine everyone here has made big decisions, sacrifices, and worked hard to reach this point.

I've loved my time in this School Counselor Education program! Reflecting on all the growth, increased professional and personal awareness, amazing friendships made, and incredible life-lessons learned over the past few years...It's my hope I might pay even a fraction of it forward by sharing some thoughts today. My time at USU has certainly been instrumental in helping me stretch in the direction of grace, gratitude, light and love.

I'm graduating today believing the following constructs and ideas, in no particular order, are pretty important:

Be intentional in recognizing and challenging implicit bias. Dare to imagine and engage in perspective taking often. If we are able to imagine another's experience, if we're willing to work to understand their perspective…that's empathy. And where there's genuine empathy, advocacy and action follow.

Equality and equity are not the same things. For many years I didn't understand this, didn't understand privilege, didn't understand the dynamics of in-group and out-group membership. I still have so much to learn. I will continue to listen, work to understand, to know and then do better.

Never pass a student in the hall without a genuine smile and greeting that communicates, "You matter, you belong here!" I understand not all of us are working in schools or with students, but this applies to any and everyone in your circle of influence. Let your people know that you've noticed them, that they matter, that they'd be missed if they weren't here.

Cognitive dissonance is information. It is also scary and uncomfortable, but if we're willing to sit with and explore it, we will learn something. One of my favorite examples of this is in the movie *The Croods* (DiMicco and Saunders 2013). Maybe some of you remember Grug (the dad) telling the story of Crispy Bear? "A long time ago this little bear was alive. She was alive because she listened to her father and lived her life in routine and darkness and terror, so she was happy." My kids find this hyperbole hilarious, but we are all likely able to relate at times—clinging to fear, never not afraid, believing what we know is what's safe, even when it's not what is best. When we stop smothering and distracting from the dissonance, when we keep exploring, keep asking questions, keep seeking the light, tomorrow is indeed brighter.

Things will seemingly happen to us, for us, because of us. There are countless eventualities we can't predict or necessarily prepare for, but I will remember one professor reminding us we can always strive to navigate each moment with emotional intelligence.

Growth mindset and mindfulness practices are game changers. I'm 38 and still working to recognize and reframe my more fixed or scarcity-mindset patterns. It is a constant work in progress, but possible. Take time to be still, be present. Life is always and only happening right now.

Look for what is right in and with the world, then work on what isn't from a place of hope and belief in abundance. Ironically enough, we talked about this idea through masks and at a time when there was plenty to find wrong with the world. We were living—are living—through our first pandemic. Yet I watched my teachers and peers continue to show up, modeling goodness, grit and hope in a brighter future they were willing to work toward. I'm so lucky for all my time spent in the company of such quality people here.

How amazing, really, that every one of us is both actively writing and trying to make sense of a story, of our story? I hope we all feel very proud of this chapter; I honor your paths that lead you to this point and wish you the very best moving forward. May we all continue to both author and interpret our stories with as much grace, gratitude, light, and love as possible.

Thank you.

(Commencement address given on May 1, 2021)

Coming full circle back to that universe-shoving-and-catching image. Sure enough, time passed, completely indifferent to what I or anyone else was doing with it, but I was proud of what I'd been a part of these past few years. I was finally finishing something I'd started over 13 years ago. I'd worked hard for this degree. My sweet kids and former husband were there supporting me. One of the ceremony photographers asked to take our picture, commenting we were a beautiful family. I couldn't agree more. I felt such gratitude to be celebrating this accomplishment with my beloved family and zero need to clarify our marital status. At the time I'd enrolled, Brandon and I were hardly speaking; what a difference three years and a lot of work makes.

I was honored to be invited to speak at graduation. It was on a run that I was thinking about these remarks, thinking about all the growth I'd both experienced and witnessed over the past few years, about the level of multitasking it took to both process our past and implement new ways of being in the present, interpreting and authoring our story—a beautifully, complicated dance. Ever onward, doing the work, trusting the universe will both shove and catch.

Rim to Rim to Rim

> Rim to Rim to Rim has been a bucket list adventure for a while. Grateful to finally run/hike/drag myself back and forth across this incredible canyon.
>
> Maybe it's recency bias, but that was one of the hardest 50-something miles I've ever done. 109 degrees at the bottom of the canyon was brutal, and a squirrel stole my favorite sour gummy worms out of my pack with 14 miles to go. It's funny today, but yesterday afternoon I was ready to cry over it.
>
> So lucky to be able to do this, and for a good friend willing to spontaneously join me! (@megbcampbell May 31, 2021)

This was quite possibly the hardest I've had to work on any adventure to not die! Rim to Rim to Rim (R2R2R) refers to the endeavor of running/hiking from one rim of the Grand Canyon to the other and back in a day. It's a serious undertaking. The park discourages traveling just rim to rim in a day, much less crossing twice. You've got to be legit prepared to make this kind of commitment—fitness, gear, planning for wide and varying contingencies. I'd canceled multiple previous attempts: once for an injured IT band that I knew wouldn't make it, other times for not wanting to miss the kids' soccer games, or opting for a desert adventure with them instead. I found a 36-hour window I could get away and decided to go for it; but I was certainly at the very end of a feasible weather window. You can really only attempt R2R2R in the fall or spring. In the winter, the north rim is covered in snow and roads are closed; in summer, the heat is deadly. This particular year, the last weekend of May was the start of a hot summer, with temperatures exceeding 100 degrees in the bottom corridor and upper 90s moving toward the rims.

I'd mentioned to my friend and colleague Marissa (one of the most incredible special education teachers I've ever had the privilege of working with and learning from) that I was planning to head to Kanab for a R2R2R attempt after school dismissed for summer break and half-jokingly asked if she wanted to join. She's a total badass, had done R2R2R before, and runs all the time, so I was only half surprised when she agreed, at least to one crossing with me. Knowing she hadn't specifically trained for this and looking at the weather, she agreed to join me for the north to south crossing, then she'd shuttle back to the North Rim when I turned around to run/hike it in reverse.

We got to Kanab Sunday night, found a little café open for dinner and luckily still serving coffee so I could take it to go and save to reheat in the morning, when nothing would be open on our way out of town. (I did learn something from that Zion's traverse close no-coffee call!) At 2:30 Monday morning we were driving to the North Rim, then running by 4AM. Our north to south crossing was pretty uneventful in the best and most beautiful of ways. By the time we were climbing up the Bright Angel trail to the South Rim, however, it was starting to really heat up. I bought some potato chips and a Sprite while Marissa coordinated her shuttle, we took a few pictures and talked through my options and plan. Originally, I wanted to run the South Rim from the Bright Angel exit over to the South Kaibab Trail and descend that route, making a lollipop of the adventure. While South Kaibab was a few miles shorter overall to the bottom of the canyon, it was more exposed, with little to no shade the entire way, and nowhere to refill water until I reached Phantom Ranch at the bottom. (Bright Angel, on the other hand, offered more shade and two rest stops with running water.) It was 96 degrees when I said goodbye to Marissa on the South Rim, and as much as I preferred a seven-mile descent over the 10 miles I had ahead of me returning the way I'd just come, Bright Angel was the smarter choice. I couldn't risk running out of water.

And then shit got really real. I was absolutely boiling, running down the South Rim, passing all kinds of carnage on the way, especially after descending past the 3-Mile Resthouse. Despite all the signage and warnings, countless tourists each year descend the canyon farther than they are able to comfortably climb themselves back out on the return. I passed people lying down in whatever shade they could find, others were throwing up along the side of the trail. To one couple with plenty of water but little fuel, I offered some electrolyte pills and applesauce squeeze pouches.

Once I passed Indian Gardens, the last water stop before Phantom Ranch at the bottom, I began running into rangers asking if I'd seen various individuals, hopefully identifiable by shirts they'd supposedly left in, whose families or friends had now reported them still somewhere in the canyon hours past their anticipated return. For how hot and miserable I felt, I was still descending. Everyone I passed was climbing, returning to the South Rim, looking significantly worse than I felt; constant reminders I still had 14 uphill miles ahead of me once I reached the Colorado River. I forced myself to focus only on the next step, the most pressing objective, and that was to arrive at Phantom Ranch before The Canteen (a convenience store on the ranch) closed for the day, because I was desperate for some ice and cold lemonade.

I arrived in time and found more park rangers, this time asking everyone planning to climb out of the canyon in either direction to please wait until at least 4PM, as it was currently 109 degrees down in that corridor. I ordered two lemonades and a large cup of ice. I shoved pieces of ice in my sports bra, down my shorts, and under my hat—I couldn't cool off fast enough. I visited with two other runners undertaking R2R2R that day, but they'd started and were finishing on the South Rim. I was so envious of their 10 remaining miles to climb in contrast to my 14. While we didn't have to wait until 4PM, it was simply a suggestion, no one was in a hurry to leave the shade of Phantom Ranch. It was brutal out on the exposed trail. In preparing for this trip, I read an account where someone had compared the blistering heat in the bottom of the canyon to a Las Vegas parking lot—heat just radiating off the ground and canyon walls. Not only was I dreading it, I was scared.

This trek out of that canyon was the first time I found my new post-divorce metrics not totally holding up. Where I used to acknowledge on long, hard runs: *This is nothing compared to divorce!* I now found myself wondering, *Nope, this really sucks, I think this is worse.* Was the pain of my divorce less salient, or was this endeavor simply that miserable and stupid?

At the start of our day, I was planning to take a short detour to see Ribbon Falls at some point—it would have only been one to two miles out of my way. It was early morning and still chilly when we passed the turnoff on our descent, but I figured the falls might be a welcome break on my return. Many hours and hellishly hot miles later, when I came again to the trail forking off toward the falls, I sighed aloud, "fucking falls." The very sign I was sure I'd look forward to reaching on my return instead irritated the crap out of me. If you know me and my love of waterfalls, my skipping a relatively nearby one is telling of how very done and spent I felt; no way was I voluntarily adding so much as an extra step to this project.

Plus, I needed to keep moving until it was safe to stop, and that meant getting back to Marissa, back to the car. The North Kaibab Trail was much quieter than the south side, so I was alone with my thoughts for most of those 14 miles up. I remember fighting some major sleepiness, willing myself to keep putting one foot in front of the other, forcing myself to stay on top of my water, salt, and food intake. I've never been so happy to get to a stream crossing and retrieve a Diet Coke Marissa had hidden under a rock in the water on our way down. I had given her a hard time, teasing that if it floated away and down to the Colorado River, she was majorly violating our leave-no-trace agreement. Now we joke that strategic Diet Coke placement saved my life!

After downing some caffeine, and as the temperature dropped, my pace naturally quickened. Later, I would very purposefully pick it way up after retrieving my headlamp from my pack at dusk only to realize it was on! I had no idea for how long it'd been on or how much battery life remained. I had to very mindfully resist the urge to panic at the thought of getting stuck out there in the dark. Couldn't believe I'd neglected to lock my headlamp when I took it off and stowed it in my pack that morning; I knew better. Time for some self-compassion and a visit to the pain cave. I was mentally and physically exhausted, but I willed myself to spin my wheel from the sensation of burning legs and screaming lungs, to a sense of resolve to keep pushing, to continue climbing faster than I felt I could. I thought about the hard we choose, the hard we're dealt, the hard we create for ourselves. I couldn't remember in my half-delirious state why I'd ever choose this R2R2R hard, but I know, whenever I find myself in the middle of it, the only way out is through.

Whenever I'm running through-the-through, writing through-the-through, attempting to work through-the-through, I'll sometimes find myself chanting, "We can't go over it. We can't go under it. Oh no! We've got to go through it!" Lines from one of our family's favorite children's books, *We're Going on a Bear Hunt* (Rosen 1989). This habit never fails to spin my wheel to happy memories of hours spent with a toddler on my lap, the book in front of us, reciting the catchy text in sing-song unison, only to reach the end and hear the sweetest little voice delightfully squeal, "again!" Granted it's not a stellar analogy if you pull too much context from the storyline—why go through the long grass, cold river, thick mud, dark forest, swirling snowstorm and gloomy cave just to disturb a bear? Still, acknowledging when it's futile to try and avoid going through something difficult is crucial for growth.

Through is how we ultimately move forward, how we overcome hard and heavy things—through ownership, through the hurt, through the miles, through lots of work—not by sidestepping around it, not by avoiding, not by disappearing (either from those you owe some restitution, or from yourself and into destructive coping behaviors). Hiding, avoiding and/or clinging to inaccurate narratives will never effectively or authentically reset anything. To eventually move on, we need to consistently show up and work through each moment to the next.

I'd once been so sure I couldn't manage another step through the divorce process, and now I felt I couldn't take another step across the Grand Canyon. When my options are keep moving or tap out...when I can't go over or under or around and realize, *oh no, I've got to go through it*...I hope I keep moving, steady and relentless, ever marveling at all the human brain, body, and soul can endure through-the-through of it all.

SOS

Since our lives don't reliably parallel themes of treasured children's books, the practice of "moving through" is far from black and white. There are occasions and individual circumstances that may sometimes prevent us from pushing through hardship—such instances are worth acknowledging and warrant compassion.

Knowing I'd have no cell phone service on my R2R2R trip, I carried my Garmin inReach device. With my inReach (a lightweight GPS and satellite communicator) I could send and receive the occasional text message, share my location with Brandon and Marissa every 20 minutes via a personal tracking link, and should I ever need to, activate an SOS that would alert a global emergency response center to coordinate my rescue.

I am pretty familiar with my limits and trusted my ability to safely complete that R2R2R endeavor. However, had I rolled an ankle, gotten dangerously sick from heat stroke, found myself out there in the dark with temperatures dropping and a dead headlamp...As stubborn as I am, I also trust I would utilize that SOS button if my safety— potentially my life—were in jeopardy.

In other situations, that SOS button has looked like reaching out to and working with a therapist or coach. For some, this SOS might be walking into an emergency room or checking into a treatment center. This is not weak, nor should it be confused with tapping out; obtaining and accepting the support needed to ultimately keep working through and moving forward is courageous.

Father's Day

> Celebrating Father's Day in some of our favorite mountains.
> Thanks, Brandon, for being a super amazing dad to our kids.
> They are truly my all-time favorite humans, and I'm so glad
> the universe knew we were meant to raise them together, not
> as married parents, but best friends. Can you even believe how
> far we've come?! I love everything about our little family so
> super much. Thanks for showing us what authentic living and
> loving looks like. (@megbcampbell June 20, 2021)

We were back in the Uinta Mountains, hiking Brandon's request of
Bald Mountain for Father's Day. (This was a little over three years
post-divorce.) Mountains always make me happy, but I remember
this particular excursion clearly, boulder hopping down the ridge,
following my kids who were following their dad that day, and I was
overwhelmed with gratitude. So grateful that we all had each other,
deeply convinced this little family was meant to be exactly as it was
right then and there. No part of me wished things were different, that
Brandon and I could have stayed married, that we could have remained
a "traditional family"—not remotely, and that awareness was still a bit
atypical at the time.

When I find myself in a moment of deep clarity, I pay attention. I
know it's often fleeting. Other hardships and distractions will later work
to tempt me out of this individual trust and knowing. I also understand
this knowing won't rescue me from the less pleasant realities of divorce
(finances suck, time management is challenging, and let's not even
talk about dating); but to have glimpses of a bigger picture, so much
bigger than I can comprehend now, yet somehow know it's bright and
beautiful and meant for me, for all of us. (I now try to put myself in the
way of these glimpses, some call them glimmers…glimmer glimpses?!
Unsurprisingly enough, the more I look, the more I find.)

These Are the Days

We've had so much fun on our first Nationals trip, but this story needs its own post.

The morning of Vi's floor event wasn't our smoothest. We took too long doing her hair, tracking down scissors to cut athletic tape and wasting time debating whether or not she had time to brush her teeth—she didn't, but was going to insist to, just not without reminding us how late we were first. I tripped and spilled coffee all over myself in our hurry to get to the venue... bit of a hot mess morning.

Violet came and found Story and me in the stands after open warmups and said, "I'm sorry I wasn't very nice this morning. I love you." No matter what happened next, I was so proud of her, acknowledging it's pretty dang hard sometimes to be stressed AND still kind, but wanting to hold both better.

I was sending her all the happy energy with major butterflies in my stomach watching her tumble. She works hard and loves this so much, it was amazing to see the day come together for her here.

I'm grateful for all she's learning in this sport, for all the ups and downs. I think/hope she's coming to value being brave and failing often enough to keep growing, in and out of tumbling. And I absolutely love the incredible team family she's gained; can't thank her coaches and sweet friends enough!

I sure love you, Vi! Keep chasing what you love, whatever that is and turns into, and I'll keep loving my front row seat. (@megbcampbell June 28, 2021)

I could talk and write about my kids' interests for days and days. Turns out I love something as random as Boston Dynamics dogs (because of Jude's fascination). I will play Grandpa Beck card games for hours (Story just doesn't tire of these). I am obsessed with power tumbling (a sport completely foreign to me until Violet, then Story, both embraced it in a big way).

I share this story to again highlight some excessive (and unnecessary) fear I was entertaining years earlier through divorce. I was so worried our kids might lose interest in or altogether abandon their beloved hobbies. I could not stand the thought of Jude not picking up his guitar again, or Violet and Story questioning their love of tumbling, or their grades totally tanking, somehow all the result of their parents' divorce?! Remember our brains are much less concerned with helping us be happy than they are with keeping us safe, and mine perceived divorce as a huge threat to myself and my family's safety, and so worried about every potential bad or sad outcome under the sun.

These concerns weren't completely unfounded or unreasonable. I knew all too well the research existed, suggesting poor outcomes for children of divorced parents. I was familiar with the well-documented correlation between divorce and kids developing social/emotional/behavioral problems. I'd observed some students start dissociating through their parents' nasty divorce, I'd watched others start acting out, their behavior as unpredictable and reckless as I can only guess their internal worlds felt. But what I needed to remember then is that those negative potentials are not inevitable; parents have a great deal of control over not only preventing those bleak outcomes, but fostering positive ones instead. (*The Truth about Children and Divorce: Dealing with the Emotions So You and Your Children Can Thrive* by Dr. Robert E. Emery [2006] is a good book to recommend here!)

Interests I once worried my kids might abandon after divorce, they instead have continued to excel in. They all work hard and do well in school, they have solid friendships, stronger relationships with both their parents after the divorce, we've gone on some of the coolest adventures together, and they're still pursuing big dreams—they have integrated a once-terrifying reality (their parents separating) into their daily lives and future goals rather seamlessly. This Nationals tumbling trip to St. Louis, Missouri, I got to witness my 11-year-old demonstrate some impressive emotional maturity and become a power tumbling national champion. I have since shed many happy tears listening to

Jude's beautiful music, watched in awe as he has led impressive rock climbing routes, and marveled at the rigorous coursework he's opted to enroll in high school. Story went on to repeat her sister's National Championships win two years later in Tulsa, Oklahoma. I followed Violet to Great Britain to watch her represent Team USA in the 2023 Trampoline and Tumbling World Age Group Competition. They've all demonstrated impressive grit and grace through countless wins and setbacks, they amaze me! How naive and even arrogant to have ever worried and wondered if divorce might taint my kids' interests or dim their passions.

And what's so much more than their accomplishments is the fact they truly are the most fun to be around, genuinely good, kind humans! Don't let fear of negative outcomes cloud all you are capable of with an open mind, gracious heart, and commitment to the work. You have so much influence as a loving, authoritative parent to continually provide kids a safe space to be and thrive.

Too Much

> A deep sense of love and belonging is an irreducible need of all women, men, and children. We are biologically, cognitively, physically, and spiritually wired to love, to be loved, and to belong. When those needs are not met, we don't function as we were meant to. We break. We fall apart. We numb. We ache. We hurt others. We get sick. (Brown 2010, 26)

Brené Brown powerfully articulates our innate need for love and belonging, and the unfortunate results of these needs going unmet. These same outcomes manifest when those love and belonging needs aren't met in a marriage. In my visits with divorcing individuals, especially in the earliest stages of divorce, there's this ever-present theme of "too much." Too much fear, too much hurt, too much uncertainty, too difficult to think clearly…it's completely overwhelming.

Whether it's you who is leaning toward leaving or your partner asking for a divorce, perhaps one of you developed a substance abuse problem in attempts to numb, or maybe it's a devastating affair that makes the decision for you; once this unraveling is set in motion, it feels entirely too much.

I remember sitting with a close friend, whose husband had just moved out, in this space of too much for the first time after my own divorce. I struggled to formulate a response, wishing I could somehow better hold the too much with her. She was right, it was too much, impossibly too much. The hurt, the anger, the despair—I felt helpless, all too familiar with the waves of sadness and heartache that would overtake her frequently, anticipating the difficult stages of grief she'd be visiting (and revisiting) in the months ahead.

I encouraged her to set those important intentions: among and between and through all the too much, decide the plan for when the ugliest versions of yourself show up. Losing control of what a former partner does now or next was feeling especially too much, but I could see her resolve to show up for her kids, to control what she could, to graciously shape her family's next steps.

I also felt a sense of, what I think you could label, survivor's guilt. I was sitting at my kitchen table, calm and regulated, sipping coffee and looking out at my beloved mountains. How did I get here? Chatting with this friend had triggered memories of a very different time—a very broken-feeling phase. Like this friend, there were months I couldn't think straight, couldn't stop crying, couldn't visualize a remotely bright future. But here I was, just watching frost melt from the grass as the sun touched it, looking forward to spending another Thanksgiving with my kids and their dad in southern Utah (one of my favorite traditions we've started since the divorce—Thanksgiving on the road and full of desert adventures) and marveling at how I arrived in this moment. How'd we survive the impossible, how'd we somehow manage to hold the "too much," without breaking under its crushing weight?

Starting the divorce paperwork was too much, telling the kids we were getting divorced was way too much, going to Brandon's brother's wedding was too much. And I'm aware there's still *too much* to come. My financial situation permanently feels like too much, me introducing the kids to a boyfriend one day will seem too much, Brandon possibly remarrying one day will be too much. But unlike five years ago, I know from experience now that I can survive the "too much." I even have a great deal of control over what the other side of too much looks like, and that's empowering.

Discussing Divorce

> It is surprisingly difficult to determine accurately the likelihood that a marriage will end in divorce, but common estimates based on census data in the United States are that 40-50% of first marriages and up to 60% of remarriages end in divorce. These rates do not account for the number of unions that break up without benefit of legal divorce. Women typically experience a 45% drop in standard of living following a divorce. Each year approximately one million children witness the dissolution of their parents' marriages and subsequently often share in their mothers' reduced circumstances. Yet divorce wrecks more than financial hardship for children. Researchers have documented increased emotional and behavioral problems, such as achievement, antisocial behavior, depression in children and adolescents after divorce. Given that divorce is sometimes the best or only alternative to a troubled marriage and that not every child of divorce suffers dire consequences, we should nonetheless consider how to help prevent what is so often a powerfully negative event in people's lives. (Broderick and Blewitt 2020, 540)

It was my first semester of graduate school, reading in my Human Development textbook. I reached chapter 13: Middle Adulthood: Cognitive, Personality and Social Development. Within this chapter was a section on divorce, full of discouraging statistics and outlining less than ideal outcomes for kids of divorced parents, like those quoted above. Brandon and I'd been divorced only five months at the time and I majorly struggled through this section. I didn't want to read these things, didn't want to know these things. I was overwhelmed with guilt and worry, and desperate to protect my kids.

Three years later I got to revisit this chapter, this time as a teaching assistant for the course and in a much more stable place to address the content. (Turns out worrying pretty excessively about divorce affecting kids results in researching pretty extensively some divorce and co-parenting best practices.) I still have so much to learn and understand and work toward, but tonight I had the opportunity to present on a topic that absolutely wrecked me three years ago. Words that were once too painful to read alone in my bedroom I discussed out loud with a class of future school counselors, and without crying!

I genuinely appreciate any chance to contribute to a hopeful change in how we (as a society) both do and view divorce, hoping one day we might see a change in these statistics and predictions…I think it will have a lot to do with grace, hope, goodwill, and love. (@megbcampbell November 30, 2021)

This post elicited the most genuine and kind response from my small Instagram circle, serving as thoughtful endorsements of my divorce story. I am overjoyed and humbled that those who witnessed Brandon and my uncoupling up close have positive and complimentary feedback.

I am also forever grateful for the opportunity to speak and share about divorcing differently, graciously, gratefully. So on that note, if you are reading this, thank you for giving the topic your valuable time!

PART 7

2022

The Journey

> I wonder if kids' amusement with our destination name contributed some to their majorly awesome attitudes today? Rumored to have been named by Butch Cassidy in honor of a girlfriend, I've been wanting to hike Ferns Nipple for a while.
>
> Big day of nearly eight miles, 3,800 feet of climbing, incredible views, and enough exposure to elicit near constant safety reminders from me.
>
> We went as far as we felt comfortable without roping kids up for the last quarter mile. We'd brought a rope and harnesses but didn't want to risk running out of daylight (or energy) on the descent.
>
> I'm so grateful for how competent and careful our kids are. I hope they're learning a healthy respect for these wild places, and how to stay safe moving through them. (@megbcampbell February 20, 2022)

Another desert adventure (in Capitol Reef National Park this time) that saw our entire unconventional family in attendance. Revisiting this post, I'm most struck by my casual mention of turning around with only a quarter mile to go, wondering at when exactly I figured out (even embraced) that whole *it's about the journey, not the destination* mentality.

I'm more typically accustomed to obsessing over destinations and outcomes and have spent most of my years relating to any goal or endeavor through an expectation I "succeed" (as defined by others or external parameters). It's been incredibly liberating to set such expectations down, to finally quiet all the scarcity self-talk. To see the destination, the peak of Ferns Nipple right before my eyes and feel no pressure to reach it—because that's not the right or responsible move under the circumstances—and grant myself permission to still experience a successful journey was evidence of remarkable progress.

Turning around so close to the top took literally nothing away from this spectacular day. In the past I would have robbed myself of all that spectacular-ness by fixating on the destination I didn't reach, a goal I didn't achieve. This same conditioning contributed to my first viewing divorce as a failure. But now I believe, just like marriage longevity doesn't indicate the success of a relationship, it's similarly unhelpful to view reaching a mountaintop or sandstone peak the metric that validates an adventure.

Simply being present with my people, moving through rugged desert wilderness, expansive red, orange, and white sandstone sprinkled green with juniper and pinyon pines in every direction, the brightest blue sky overhead. Sharing this experience of feeling so small, so alive, so close to one another and to nature is special. It's why we keep returning. Not to reach new and box-checking destinations, but to experience that magnificent connection, to marvel at what we're a part of.

Mad, Sad, Frustrated and Stressed

I'm sitting in my kitchen on the verge of tears, sending another text to good friends, just a few months after the last: "I can't go to Moab this weekend." What I don't get into is how I plain and simple can't afford it.

This morning I'm simply mad and sad and frustrated and stressed. I'm mad at how messed up education is and how screwed our country is because we won't invest in it better. I've worked in the field for over 13 years now and am planning to until what's sure to be a very late retirement. Loving the work, which I do, doesn't make up for the living expenses I simply can't meet some months.

Just think of your favorite teacher, or maybe it was a school counselor or principal who greatly influenced your life and trajectory. They are compensated so poorly. Even with a master of education degree, my earning potential is capped depressingly low. It was disheartening to realize, ironically enough in a graduate-level career counseling course, that I would be set up to make more money with much less student loan debt had I pursued a career in welding, cosmetology, or dental hygiene— literally just about any and everything else. Ugh.

I'm not dismissing the huge importance of finding purpose and value in your work, but it shouldn't be so damn hard for educators to support themselves and a family. When I first pursued this career path, it was an ideal "mom major"—I'd get married, teach for a couple years, have kids, be a stay-at-home mom, that was the plan. While I remain grateful that I was brave enough to deviate, I didn't and haven't set myself up for financial stability, much less success. (Journal entry from May 2022)

Well, that was an ornery entry. I'm including it with the hope this book adequately highlights that such instances of sadness and frustration will be plentiful post-divorce. I can't think of anything that's a work-through-it-once-and-you're-set kind of thing. I had a good cry, then forced myself to breathe into and through the big emotions. I regulated and returned to some peaceful knowing of not wanting to trade my current circumstances for anything. My life was real and honest, I was part of the happiest and healthiest relationships I've ever known, I was living in line with core values, and that's worth more than the money I was so stressed over not having.

Still, I needed to figure out some next steps. Month after month, the insufficient funds, overdraft protection advance, and negative account balance notices induced stressful, sinking feelings. It wasn't responsible, it wasn't sustainable; I knew this. When I tried to problem solve from a place of love and abundance—versus scarcity and fear— another reminder from my LDS days returned.

CTR: Choose the Right

I grew up with CTR postcards in my room, CTR rings on my finger. In the LDS faith, CTR stands for Choose the Right. I wore the rings but personally never loved the reminder; it felt too big-brotherish, too much of a warning. I knew the answer to "or else" and the shame that came with that...it just felt yucky.

It was during a church youth conference at some impressionable point of my adolescence, a speaker provided an additional option for our CTR acronym: Character, Truth, Relationships. Sure, he tied character to important Mormon-defining traits I no longer endorse, truth to the faith he reminded us we were so blessed to be members of, relationships to the ones we should cherish most (those with our Heavenly Father and Savior), but he also contrasted these constructs with material items like money, clothes, toys—literal things that you can't take with you, things that will hold minimal or no significance once you're gone.

When integrated through a non-dogmatic mindset, I appreciate this CTR reminder now. At any intersection where I'm tempted by scarcity, by asshat-selfishness, by "things," I explore questions like, *Will this matter in two months, two years, twenty years? How will this affect my character? What about my relationships? What is true?* Divorce doesn't have to cost anyone their character, their truth, their treasured relationships (even if/when some relationships will look very different, like a spouse to co-parent one). It's a choice and practice to value these abstract, enduring things more than the physical ones we're often concerned with winning through divorce.

187

Divorce impacts and often resets any financial plans in big ways. I can understand how and why it's tempting to get aggressive over resources. I would plead with anyone in the middle of those difficult dividing of money and resources conversations and decisions: Do what it takes to get objective about what is right/correct/fair, then move forward, making lifestyle changes accordingly. Forever fighting over money and things will turn you into a tiny-hearted human.

Circling back to my once-steady stream of distressing bank statements…I am slowly but surely getting a handle on the state of my finances! This is largely the result of me finally and vulnerably reaching out to Brandon and asking for more monetary support than our divorce decree initially outlined. His response, "Of course, whatever you need," and within the minute a notification appeared on my phone, informing me that money had been transferred to my checking account and the balance was available to use. Brandon took over girls' tumbling tuition payments, he covers our family membership to the local climbing gym, provides our kids with whatever equipment they need to participate in the activities they love (all in addition to monthly child support), and never once have I heard him make a snide or exasperated comment about money.

Brandon and I reached a place, years post-divorce, where I communicated a need, he agreed it was valid, and we collaborated on a new arrangement. I believe this was possible because we refused to ever fight over money or things in the beginning. We never allowed money to become an enormous source of contention, so we are able to peacefully re-evaluate what is equitable now, what makes sense now, what is best for kids now. Brandon and I trust each other to always and unequivocally prioritize our kids, and understand that continuing to support one another (whatever that looks like over the course of co-parenting together) serves to also support those precious kids.

Earlier I suggested, do what it takes to get clear about what is financially fair, and stop fighting. I would also advise, as a next step, do what it takes to earn and establish trust with your co-parent, that if or when you do reach out for additional help, they feel safe assuming it is from a genuine place. (Don't use a seemingly child-centered pretense to manipulate your former partner in an attempt to gain more. Don't compromise your character, don't bend the truth, don't ruin what could be a vibrant co-parenting relationship.)

Moving On

What does it even mean to move on? I suppose in the most obvious sense we are all always moving on, as time is never not. A fact that's all too easy to forget and accounts for the kind of reminders I've either tried to inspire or maybe just torture myself with in the past:

> *The cleaning and scrubbing can wait til tomorrow, but children grow up as I've learned to my sorrow. So quiet down cobwebs, dust go to sleep. I'm rocking my baby, and babies don't keep.* This poem was given to me at a baby shower. I'd rehearse it in my head, nursing and rocking all three of my little babies.

> *The days are long, the years short...* With this reminder I'd try to force myself to appreciate the sleepless nights, embrace the zombie-like state I occupied through the newborn phases, and be grateful for the irate toddler screaming at me in the grocery store when time seemed to be crawling.

> *There is a last time for everything...One day you will carry your child on your hip then set them down, and never pick them up that way again. You will scrub their hair in the bath one night, and from that day on they will want to bathe alone. They will hold your hand to cross the road, then never reach for it again. They will creep into your room at midnight for cuddles, and it will be the last time you ever wake to this. The thing is, you won't ever know it's the last time, until there are no more times.* Okay, this one still just makes me cry. When I first stumbled across it late one night scrolling my phone when I should have been sleeping myself, I raced downstairs to hold Jude, who was

sound asleep. He must have been 7 or 8 years old. I still held his younger sisters plenty but couldn't recall the last time I'd held him and had to ensure I hadn't missed it.

There are only 940 Saturdays between a child's birth and their leaving for college. I'm at half those Saturdays with Story, much less with Jude and Violet. Dang, it goes fast!

I suppose it's a fine line between integrating these reminders as helpful and healthy versus harmful and guilt-inducing; regardless, I've devoured them.

Upon first learning I was pregnant with Jude, I felt so ill-prepared to be a mom, to be a good mom. I read dozens of parenting books, all the advice, all the quotes. Later in life, particularly through my divorce, I turned again to literature, sought advice, devoured all legit-seeming suggestions. The content now often alluded to themes of different potential regret: realizing late in life that you're out of time, that you never did the work, never tried to better understand yourself or why and how you show up in relationships, never attempted to address and process past pain, never risked being truly seen and known.

I'm still in and working through this moving-on-after-divorce phase. Sheesh, it's complicated and intimidating! (Wish I could just insert that shoulder-shrugging, heck-if-I-know emoji here—it's about the best response I've got to the question and idea of moving on.) Shortly after my divorce I noticed a heightened sense of urgency to move on, definitely developed a bit of "hurry sickness" to heal quickly, and felt rushed to be more okay right away. Now I understand that pressing and painful need to feel safe fast is a trauma response. I recognize in hindsight my desperation and neediness to be okay—to want to feel better immediately and to look for that everywhere but inside myself—was the result of things like those exposed Swiss cheese holes, a reflection of various needs never met, a misunderstood and long-ingrained disorganized attachment style. For many of us, by the time we leave a marriage, we're hauling around so much childhood, adult, and relational baggage, it's a mystery we're able to remain relatively high functioning at all.

Since young adulthood, I've tried to skip, distract, and/or just stay crazy-busy enough to stay ahead of the hurt, the truth, the work. I've made some shitty choices and regrettable mistakes trying to escape myself. I've further hurt myself and others trying to avoid the real work of reflecting, changing, healing. We know there are no shortcuts if you hope to one day be and feel honestly whole. All those voids I was desperate for another to fill, I had to figure out how to fill those myself. The many nights I couldn't stand to be alone, I had to sit through alone. The few distracting situationships I was in a hurry to explore, predictably imploded, only prolonging the inevitable work.

I've grown fascinated with attraction theory. It makes sense we attract the intentions and energy we're emitting ourselves, that we're drawn to other, similar frequencies—healthy tends to attract healthy, dysfunction gravitates toward other dysfunction, fear seems to chase and trigger more fear. It also stands to reason that the relationships we pursue will reveal work still to be done, places we still need to heal, and that who we're drawn and attracted to will change once we begin to love ourselves better. This self-love results from exploring the dark corners, addressing our own red flags, and changing patterns of behavior that are keeping us stuck.

For some, this may include reparenting work, working with a trauma-informed therapist to bring the unconscious to conscious, exploring and addressing core beliefs and habits that have been influencing (perhaps sabotaging) your relationships. Or maybe your next steps don't require clinical support, but you'd benefit from help in better understanding and managing expectations, setting and honoring important boundaries, learning to listen and communicate more effectively—it doesn't happen overnight, and I'd be skeptical of anyone trying to convince you otherwise. (Dr. Nicole LePera's book *How to Do the Work* [2021] is an approachable resource for anyone looking for somewhere to start!)

Again, this all serves to highlight why parenting through divorce is so difficult. It's okay to not be okay, but don't fall completely apart in front of your kids. It's odd and inauthentic to be "fine" right away, but don't ask your kids to hold your adult problems. Sit with heartache, uncertainty, and grief while also reassuring your kids that you're still a family, you'll never leave them, they're forever and unconditionally loved. Maybe modeling a healthy "moving on" is the hardest ask of all. But if we agree it's worth the hard, worth the work, worth navigating *through* all the gray area to be intentional about how we model moving on in front of our kids, we should discuss moving on and into new romantic relationships.

It will always be a big adjustment for kids to see their mom or dad with a new romantic partner, but to be obligated to face and process it during or immediately after their parents' divorce is asking a lot. Kids are already being forced to integrate excessive change; chances are they didn't readily welcome or want these new circumstances. They need their parents' presence now more than ever. Kids need their parents to be both physically and emotionally available to hold all the heavy and uncertain newness with them. As much as you may think you're able to manage it, you really can't effectively show up for kids in this capacity, heal from divorce yourself, continue meeting the demands of your professional life, and invest in a new relationship all at the same time—at least not a healthy one—and I'm okay occasionally standing alone in this opinion.

I know, I know...I've been accused of being judgmental, of not understanding self-care, of discouraging simple pleasure after years of an unhappy marriage. Absolutely we all want to feel seen, want to feel noticed, want to feel wanted again; I just urge parents to also be cognizant of how your timing here affects kids. Introducing new partners during or just after divorce further disrupts the family system, a system already strained by and feeling countless repercussions of an ending marriage. Family Systems Theory proposes that "families so profoundly affect their members' thoughts, feelings, and actions that it often seems as if people are living under the same 'emotional skin.' People solicit each other's attention, approval, and support, and they react to each other's needs, expectations, and upsets. This connectedness and reactivity make the functioning of family members interdependent" (The Bowen Center, n.d.).

The relationship minor children have with their parents is central and primary. When a parent pursues a new romantic relationship, it is difficult to give those primary relationships with kids the time, energy, and attention they need—especially if/when that secondary relationship is intoxicating and consuming, as new love interests often are. When a secondary relationship (new boy/girlfriend) takes priority over a primary one (parent-child) during or just following divorce, that's confusing and painful for the child, who is likely extra dependent on and needing the safety of that primary connection with their parent through an already-big disruption to the family system.

In *The Truth About Children and Divorce*, when referencing new love interests post-divorce, Dr. Emery advises: "...Another lesson you will need to learn is patience. If you do not want to divorce your children as well as your spouse, you will need to plan to rebuild your relationship with them as a single parent before you introduce someone new into your life and theirs" (2006, 130).

Six to twelve months. Kate (my uncoupling coach) suggested a minimum of six months post-divorce of not entertaining or pursuing any romantic relationships. Sure, it does and should vary on an individual basis, but six months was a reasonable ask for me. At least six months of feeling it all, being available for and adjusting to all the newness with the kids, investing in those primary relationships, resetting and grounding myself as a newly single parent to move on from a more stable place.

•••••━━━━━━━━━•━━━━━━━━━•••••

I have visited with enough divorcing individuals to understand how/why this section in particular may bring up some anger, defensiveness and/or feelings of regret. Sometimes regret is instructive, other times it's pointlessly painful and mindless. I never want these words to be or feel weaponized against anyone. It's never too late to reset, to do something differently today than you've done in the past, to tune in, determine what this moment needs, and do that. This might look like a vulnerable conversation with your kids, maybe even an apology...

"I'm sorry I wasn't more available, I'm sorry if you felt alone or had needs I wasn't meeting. I want to do better. Can we talk about it?" (It's powerful when parents model taking ownership and ask what they can do to repair a relationship. Even if your child is unsure how to respond at first, continue opening the door for meaningful conversations.)

Or perhaps you did the very thing I've advised against, re-coupling during or just after divorce, and my words are landing somewhere between mildly irritating to downright infuriating. It's understandable if you can't agree with or remotely endorse this content because the opposite has worked out wonderfully for you and your family. While such examples are more the minority, I do know they exist, and am genuinely happy for all involved! If this section (or any of the material in this memoir, for that matter) has come across offensive, I hope you take comfort in knowing your own heart best, knowing your family system best, knowing you did your best with the tools you had and the hand you were dealt, and things have worked out as they should, which is the best kind of knowing.

It is my sincere hope for all of us that we don't spend too much precious time looking back; our kids are not growing in that direction, life isn't moving that way. I find myself randomly contemplating this idea on trail runs—constantly hopping tree roots, carefully placing my steps in between rocks, leaping over standing water or running streams—can you imagine trying to do this, make forward progress, while facing backward?! Not only would it be horribly inefficient, but also physically dangerous. The same is true for our spiritual state, it's both unhelpful and unhealthy to be stuck in or perma-ruminating on the past.

Moving On...?

I mentioned my uncoupling coach suggested I wait at least six months after divorce before entertaining the idea of a new romantic relationship. I've since wondered, and had well-meaning friends question, if it's possible to stretch that recommendation out for far too long. In my case, at the time I'm writing this, those six months have turned into over five years, and I'm still not totally sure where I stand on the whole idea of recoupling. I've participated in some dysfunctional friend/situationships, walked right into obvious dead ends, have been fooled by masterful manipulators, then gone on to hurt others with my unwillingness to get too real, risk too much, get too close to potential big hurt again.

For a while, I was rather jaded on the whole idea of marriage especially. I'd engage in confirmation bias and validate my pessimism with reading about how unnatural monogamy is. Even other mammals we call monogamous are mostly just seasonally monogamous, not lifelong partners. My friend Kari was quick to point out that we're also the only mammals with highly developed frontal cortices, so that's a lame comparison, hardly supporting an already weak argument. I've conceded the idea that "marriage sets us up to fail" isn't totally fair, but perhaps the healthiest relationships are based on some variation of "let's be together for as long as we both want to be together, for as long as we enhance each other's happiness, for as long as we honestly choose each other."

There was a time I was also drawn to the idea of happy lobsters, from my *Friends* (Burrows 1996) obsession days when Phoebe referred to Ross and Rachel as lobsters, meant to be together forever. I recently went to rewatch that clip, and in my search for it, the internet rudely informed me that lobsters do not, in fact, mate for life. They are monogamous for only about two weeks, and male lobsters are rather promiscuous in between those periods. What?!

Nevertheless, I won't deny I like the thought of someone that I want to do all the ups and downs and beautiful and terrible moments with. Neither of us ignorantly believing the other can meet and/ or fulfill all our needs, jointly understanding we are responsible for ourselves, both committed to continuing our individual work, then actively and intentionally choosing to support each other, to join our paths, to work through the losses and celebrate the wins together. If I'm being perfectly honest, that's the dream; I've just taken very few steps toward it.

A number of plans I've thought were pretty brilliant in theory plain sucked in practice. At one point, a few years after my divorce, I entertained the idea of getting on a dating app. I was skeptical, but tried to convince myself it was "fine" and is, after all, how you meet people "these days." I entered very minimal info, uploaded a few photos, and went to bed. I awoke the next morning to dozens of notifications, apparently mistaken in my assumption that my profile was private (turns out you had to pay for that feature). I fumbled my phone a number of times in my hurry to completely erase everything. The quicker I deleted my account, the quicker I could pretend that just the thought of an actual date with any of these men wasn't terrifying. I wasn't ready.

I did meet someone organically, running a half marathon, who interested-without-frightening me. Also divorced and exploring this idea of moving on himself, he'd ever so gently call out some of my delusional relationship ideas. I was longing for connection but looking for it from a safe distance. Anything real will also be vulnerable, making *happy connection from a safe distance* a total oxymoron. I remember him commenting, still relatively early in our getting to know each other, but exploring an initial and mutual attraction: "I am getting to know you, enjoying your attention and your mind…I am also walking headfirst into a woman who is terrified of anything real, so I wouldn't say this is intelligent for me."

Wrecked and rescued. While that particular connection did not ultimately evolve into more, it was eye-opening. I don't want to be terrified of anything real forever. Even throughout our divorce, Brandon and I shared a future hope that our kids might one day see their parents model healthy romantic relationships, genuine and safe connections with another, authentic partnerships—things the two of us together couldn't show them.

I've so badly wanted to avoid any more hurt, any further disruption of my kids' lives, any more scary uncertainty. I've also needed this time to finally learn how to be alone, to understand I am solely responsible for myself, to trust I can, in fact, be happy without another human to validate my existence or day-to-day experiences. Plus, this time has allowed Brandon and I to establish a friendship and co-parenting relationship I'm not sure would have been possible had either of us "moved on" right away. So, for those reasons I am grateful, but also recognizing that being single is not what I want forever.

Wanting more will mean I need to put myself out there more. I'm not totally sure what that looks like, it's wild. I've done so much work, grown a ton, am finally comfortable with and confident in *me*, but when I engage at all with an interested guy, I am triggered left and right. Figuring out how to trust myself to trust another human with all the good, lovely, raw, and ugly parts of me…figuring out how to hold space and embrace the good, lovely, raw and ugly parts of another…I have no illusions it'll be easy, but I feel myself moving toward a place of wanting to choose that hard next. One reminder that's currently helping the most with any and all forms of moving on is Nelson Mandela's beautiful wisdom: "May your choices reflect your hopes, not your fears" (n.d.). Both difficult and incredible to fathom what all our relationships would look like if we were brave enough to practice that.

Letting Go

Pretty sure moving on in any capacity will always also include a lot of letting go.

"Mom, Luca invited me to go to Flaming Gorge—camping, river rafting, boating—sounds way fun!" Jude exclaimed.

"For how long?" I asked.

"Til Wednesday, so like four days," Jude responds, and my chest tightens.

"Oh no, that's too long, I don't think so."

"I think it'd be a lot of fun, I'd really like to go, but I understand if you want me to stay home." He's sincere, a little sad, a little hopeful.

Oh crap. I've screwed up somewhere. I can hear Jude feeling responsible for me, for the comfort level and well-being of his mom. My 12-year-old is approaching me with a reasonable request and already conceding to my probable unreasonable answer.

For so long, I'd used my kids to justify remaining married. Then, through and after the divorce, showing up for them, protecting them, loving them became my all-consuming plan. In many ways this served us well, but my over-interest was likely perceptible to the kids, and at some point, they started to internalize the idea they were at least a little responsible for me in return.

My kids didn't choose me for their mom, nor do they owe me anything. I feel lucky to occupy this rock at the same time as these fantastically amazing, unique, beautiful humans. And I hope to build relationships with them that continue to enhance all our individual lives. Jude, Vi, and Story do this for me a million times over every single day; the joy they bring me is a happy outcome of our relationships, but they aren't in charge of ensuring it.

"You're right, I'm sorry, you should totally go," I answered.

"Are you sure? Will you be okay?" Jude is part thrilled, part skeptical.

I thanked him for caring and did my best to explain and reassure him that he doesn't need to worry about me, that I'm sorry I've made him feel the need to. I told him how much I love his easy-going, fun-loving nature and think it's great he's so quick to jump at the chance to join an adventure, while also thinking to myself, *Don't you dare condition this out of him.* He thanked me, started packing, and I made sure to keep any excessive comments about how much I'd miss him to myself. Two days into his trip I got this text: *I have service in the middle of the lake. I am doing awesome. Can't wait to tell you all about it!*

I don't think my kids have ever felt they needed to take care of me necessarily. They would agree I'm pretty independent, capable, and certainly stubborn. They were happy enough to let me change my first flat tire post-divorce (with the help of YouTube), they rarely insist on shoveling snow before I get to it (imagine that), they'll occasionally try to talk me into putting their laundry away (nice try); they trust me to figure out or problem solve most things. But I also know they've felt some sense of responsibility for my simply being okay while apart from them. For a long time they would ask what I was going to do when they were headed off with their dad, wanting to confirm I'd be able to fill my solo hours.

Violet once asked what I'd do when they were all moved out and off to college. Story chimed in, "She'll probably sit in our rooms and cry." We all laughed. I joke about it now because I can tell the concern they once felt over my being alone and okay has naturally lessened as I've grown genuinely better at being alone and okay. That's not to say Story's prediction isn't accurate; I will absolutely sit in their childhood bedrooms and cry on occasion, spend a few moments with lovely memories, feel immense gratitude to be their mom, send lots of concentrated unconditional love and light their way, then continue about my day. Holding on and letting go simultaneously, over and over again.

Dead Baby Deer

> In our saddest moments, we want to be held by or feel connected to someone who has known that same ache, even if what caused it is completely different. We don't want our sadness overlooked or diminished by someone who can't tolerate what we're feeling because they're unwilling or unable to own their own sadness. (Brown 2021, 109)

"I saw the saddest thing yesterday. There was a dead baby deer on the side of the road. It must have recently been hit, its mom was standing over it, nudging it with her nose." Jude shared this somber recollection early one fall morning when I was driving him and Vi to school, Story also in the car with us, along for the ride since her elementary school started 40 minutes later.

It was quiet for a few moments. I was waiting for Violet to shriek, "Don't talk about it!" That's been a common response of hers in the past, refusing to engage in sad topics, especially involving animals. We all know that instinct, desperate to shut sadness out, hoping if we don't speak it, we won't feel it. As a kid, I hated watching *Bambi* and *The Land Before Time*. I felt so restless having to sit through young Bambi and Littlefoot losing their mothers. I didn't know how to hold the feelings those scenes elicited, and it was physically uncomfortable. I could see Story on the verge of tears in the rearview mirror, processing Jude's uncomfortable comment. But she didn't say anything, and a reactive outburst from Violet never came.

"That is really sad," I responded. "A dead baby deer is sad, its mom hoping she will nudge it awake is sad. It's something that will always be sad and nothing will make it less sad. You feel sadness over sad things because your hearts are so good, because you're noticing, you're present, because you're willing to feel both hard and happy feelings. I love how you all love animals, love that you value life. Even though this is hard and doesn't feel good, I hope we always feel sadness when we witness something sad, and I'm glad we can talk about it. We can feel sad together."

Five years ago, this conversation would have gone very differently. I would have shied away from discussing hard or sad things, I would have tried to distract the kids or find some silver lining. There's no denying that divorce and all that's followed has taught me to own my sadness. Sadness, like any and every emotion, is a condition of existence.

Sometimes now, when we witness or experience something sad, one of us may comment, "It's a dead baby deer"—immediately that sadness is validated, recognized, and held together. If I'd had this analogy five years ago, I would have acknowledged with my kids that divorce is a dead baby deer. Nothing could or would make it feel better or okay or remotely less sad for a while. Sometimes holding and loving each other through sadness is all there is to do.

Wasatch 100

Took me three sleeps and a chat with the amazing Katy Blommer to start processing my Wasatch experience. I've always loved my trail time, but started running longer distances 4-5 years ago through my divorce. I registered for the Bear 100 when Brandon and I were filing the paperwork that'd dissolve our marriage. Six months later, I called my finish there lucky, but also went on to make some important agreements with myself to not glorify or value pointless suffering moving forward—not in running, not in relationships, not in everyday life... which left me super conflicted at Wasatch.

Trail running has always been a sort of therapy—cheaper than actual therapy (which I'm a big advocate of, just not always the most affordable), and it's healthier than some other coping options. Over the years, my running has evolved from an escaping/distracting outlet to a genuine self-care practice. I really wanted to run another hundred-miler in this more stable place and mindset; it just wasn't meant to be this weekend.

By mile 50ish, we were way behind schedule and the minor head cold I'd started with had moved to my lungs. I was miserable. That's to be expected, regardless, to some extent; but my inability to stop shivering or slow my racing heart rate, and being scared at how difficult it was becoming to breathe had me ready to abandon any and all plans. I came into Brighton (around mile 70) resolved to drop, listen to my body, get some sleep, avoid getting so sick I couldn't show up for kids' stuff and work this week. Any other day in the mountains, these calls are easier to make, but race day and in my delirious state, I started second-guessing myself. Maybe I wasn't that sick, maybe I could keep going, and on this went until mile 90. Every step felt horribly irresponsible; I didn't trust my ability to stay safe out there (again, violating some big agreements with myself).

The sweet aid station workers at mile 90 kept insisting I had plenty of time to waddle, crawl, roll downhill to the finish, and I knew Marissa could get me there, but I felt compelled to honor the decision I believed should have been made 20-plus miles and countless hours ago. I apologized to Marissa for my being such a mess, apologized to my body for not listening sooner, and asked for the drop form. First DNF (did not finish) was pretty bittersweet. I wish I'd committed to it sooner, dropped at Brighton and made it back for Jude's bike race and girls' soccer games. Gotta love the mom regret that comes with 20/20 hindsight, but also proud of myself for ultimately choosing and listening to me—something that's taken a lot of work.

The disappointment, however, that also comes with this DNF is new and not at all fun to hold—effing sucks, actually—but then my sweet friend Sammi drops off a favorite reminder (a large, framed print of Man in the Arena speech) that to fail means you first showed up and tried for something, so I'm embracing it. Thanks to everyone who made my Wasatch attempt possible and my tribe of sweet friends and family, especially my kids, who coming home to makes everything better. (@megbcampbell September 13, 2022)

Wasatch 100 is a point-to-point 100-mile endurance run that traverses the central Wasatch Mountain Range of Utah with about 24,000 feet of climbing. So many beautiful and difficult takeaways from this one. When I was recounting the whole thing in detail to Katy, after patiently listening, she asked me to back up. (Katy is a master at helping identify first steps and patterns in self-abandonment habits.) We backed way up to when I'd asked a friend if they wanted to train for and run this with me.

My first 100-miler (The Bear) four years earlier, I was running away from so much. I wanted to return to this distance no longer running from, but now toward, myself. (Cause how poetic is that?!) For how too attached I was to this goal to begin with, I set myself up for some disappointment by outsourcing it. In asking a friend to run with me, I gave away some important control over executing my own race. I don't fault or blame this friend, not remotely, it was my idea. (Trusting myself is an area that still needs some work.)

I woke up at 3:30AM race-day morning, opened the basement door to let the dogs out, and the smell of smoke was overwhelming. I reached for my phone and pulled up the air quality index. My heart sank to see the Wasatch range covered in dots ranging from yellow and orange to red and deep purple, indicating just how poor of air we'd be breathing for the next 30-plus hours. I didn't have time to look up what western US fire was responsible for the smoke I was inhaling, just knew this was bad timing.

WITH GRACE AND GRATITUDE

The friend I was running with has asthma, and the poor air quality (understandably) slowed our planned pace down almost immediately. Mile after mile, I grew increasingly concerned. I was prepared to be out there for 28–32 hours, not more. By 40 miles in, we were already over three hours behind our planned pace, and I was painfully aware I was missing my window to have a hard conversation and discuss splitting up.

By midnight, when I should have been arriving at the aid station where all my warm clothes were waiting, I was miles away—unable to regulate my body temperature with a pace that'd keep me warm—I was shivering uncontrollably and absolutely freezing up at 10,000 feet on a high Wasatch ridge. It would be another three and a half hours before I reached that crew bag of warmer gear, and by then I was miserably cold, sick, and wholly unwell. I can't say or know what would have happened had I spoken up when I felt strong and needed to be moving faster those first 50 miles. I do know that I talked myself into walking, waiting, being a "good friend." These are things I'm happy to do and embrace on any other adventure; others have done the same for me countless times—the comradery of the ultra-trail running community is incredible. But on 100-mile race day, those things required me to ignore some individual understanding: *You can't sustain this, you are moving too slow, you are too cold, this is unsafe.*

No part of this race had resembled what I'd set out to do in the first place. I'd regressed to old habits of staying quiet, not asking for what I need, talking myself out of prioritizing my plans and goals to keep others comfortable. In the past, I may have resented my friend, like I resented Brandon year after year of our marriage. We come to resent anyone ignoring the needs we aren't communicating; we inevitably project and find an outlet for our frustration. But I knew better now.

I was disappointed in myself for unrealistic planning; training and starting with my friend, then knowing we supported however the other's race evolved would have been much wiser. I was disappointed in myself for not speaking up from mile 6 to mile 50, and everywhere in between. I was disappointed in myself for not withdrawing at mile 70 when I knew that was the right call. I was disappointed that I once again talked myself down a path my core wasn't invested in. In this case, that path involved 20 more miles with a ton of elevation gain, and I dreaded nearing the finish.

At first, I couldn't make sense of this dread and confliction in the context of a trail race, yet it was familiar. I was allowing incongruence; my insides and outsides didn't match. I was at war with myself out there. Customarily I would insist on finishing (like I had at The Bear), but I could recognize those inclinations coming from an older version of me; a very obstinate version that let scarcity mentality drive decisions: *I'm not a quitter, I have to finish what I start, what would people think, giving up is weak, what would I tell everyone?!* For many years my worth and value were so intricately tied up in appearances, performances, and achievements; I had to deliver. While I experienced major discomfort around the idea of quitting, I forced myself to keep entertaining it. Whatever version of me I was on at Wasatch felt strongly that to finish would feel dishonest and out of line with values I'd been working hard to honor lately.

Mile 90 was my last chance to drop, my last shot at a DNF form before the finish line, where then it's obviously too late. It's difficult to explain and sounds so backward, but after all the disappointment of the past 90 miles and 30-plus hours, I knew I'd feel most disappointed to finish. Priorities had shifted, both out there in that race and over the past five years in my life. I'd adamantly decided to stop celebrating or participating in pointless suffering, enduring just for the sake of enduring because you *should*, especially when it comes at the expense of listening to your core and/or your health (physical, mental, emotional, or otherwise). That's not a practice I want to willfully waste more time on. At Wasatch, these relatively newfound values were being tested in a big arena.

One hundred miles is a big commitment; I'd been training for months, race registration was a significant financial commitment, many people had rearranged their schedules to come support me, and I was missing the kids' Saturday activities. What reasons are heavy or valid or plentiful enough to finish, to outweigh core knowing that I needed to drop out? I could compare it to sticking it out in a marriage

WITH GRACE AND GRATITUDE

that had run its course. What reasons are heavy or valid or plentiful enough to stay married, to outweigh core knowing I needed to get divorced? Turns out I did have some practice with hard questions.

I sat under the tent of the mile 90 aid station, feverish and hacking to the point of heaving while I completed my first DNF form. I knew it was the right decision, but that knowing didn't protect me from the wave of sadness and worry that followed. Listening to myself also meant I had a lot to answer for elsewhere. I was dreading trying to explain this, dreading all the celebratory finish posts, dreading the recognition of others' grit that I didn't have or couldn't demonstrate.

Unexpected Takeaways

I spent a few restless nights ruminating over what I'd chalked up to be a total disaster. Then I'd feel sorry for myself because this was supposed to be a redemption run of sorts. I'd even outlined the chapter in my head (big mistake, as I know expectations are dangerous). The glamorous idea of returning to a challenge I once took on from such a broken place to run it more whole, but instead it was an absolute shitshow, a dead baby deer, downright sad.

I tried to remain honest and vulnerable, tried to accept each moment as if I'd chosen it, and in the days and weeks that followed, the coolest things happened. I chose to quit instead of finish something, because in this instance that resolved some incongruence. I chose to redirect from a path and plan that no longer felt right; I chose to trust me. In the past, I would have died of embarrassment over a DNF result, but guess what? I didn't die, my world didn't end. The people who I love most still loved me back; better yet, they were there to hold some sadness and disappointment with me and made it abundantly clear no running success or failure could touch their love for and acceptance of me.

Wasatch didn't go as planned or look anything like I'd envisioned and hoped, but maybe I didn't need to prove that I was hard or tough enough to run and finish a strong 100-miler. Maybe I needed to learn I could risk falling short of a goal, risk quitting, risk possibly disappointing others to show up for myself. Yes, the immediate aftermath was very unpleasant, but the values honored and learning that resulted was priceless. More parallels here between my Wasatch attempt, my divorce, the ultramarathon of life; maybe all the learning is always the point, maybe we should celebrate opportunities to demonstrate growth, even when it initially looks and feels like failure. Give yourself some time and space to recognize the wins emerge from the falls, they're easier to spot when you remain soft and open.

While working through a few final citation edits, I found this section still a little uncomfy to revisit, still felt a twinge of embarrassment. I opened Instagram—to review my original Wasatch post—then, serendipitously enough, found myself engrossed with the content at the top of my feed: "Some of the worst advice is to never quit. Or don't ever give up. Knowing when to quit and move on takes true self-awareness…Wise people let go when they need to" (LePera 2024). A sweet wreck-and-rescue reassurance from the universe.

I'm currently registered for another Wasatch 100 attempt, next September, 2024. I'm preparing with some Working Mom Happiness Method wisdom: take messy action (chase this goal in a deliberately non-perfect way), go in with HILA (high intentions, low attachment), routinely check in with and trust myself, and I'm already nothing but grateful for however this second attempt unfolds (because stepping outside my comfort zone and pursuing something I feel excitement toward is a privilege). Wish me luck!

Half Dome

Half Dome!! I finally got permits and am still marveling at how fantastically lucky that my favorite humans will join me on these adventures.

Between trail closures and needing to park at a lower trailhead it turned into an 18-mile day with about 6,000 feet of climbing. Longest single day effort for all three kids and they absolutely rocked it…Seriously, I get emotional over how much I love this time together.

Jude clipped himself into the cables. We roped Violet to Brandon and Story to me. About 200 feet from the top, Story asked if we could please turn around. (The cable section is no joke steep and her little feet were slipping out from under her almost every step.) She may not share my summit-fever, but I love that she'll speak up and embrace her Granddad's wisdom: don't go up anything you don't trust you can get yourself safely back down. We ask so much of her on these hikes, treat her like a big kid, forgetting she probably has to take two to three steps for every one of ours, her little arms shaking with a death-grip on those cables…No way was I making her ask twice. We descended to the sub-dome and soaked in the amazingness.

I knew Jude would insist on going to the top regardless. I wasn't sure what Vi would choose, but she decided to go for it. I know it took some major mindfulness for her to keep carefully placing and trusting every step. So proud of all of them! Happy bubble day! (@megbcampbell October 11, 2022)

Over four years now since that precedent-setting Uinta backpacking trip and we're still adventuring together as a family! This time it was up the iconic Half Dome in Yosemite National Park. The final section of this climb involves ascending 400 feet of very steep granite. The park has installed two lines of hand cables here, allowing hikers to reach the summit without traditional rock climbing gear. The consequences of a slip off the cables though are fatal, so Brandon and I had decided we'd all wear our climbing harnesses for this stretch. Jude tied into a short rope himself and clipped the other end (secured to a carabiner) onto the cables. The girls were safely tied to Brandon or me, and we were practicing the same cable clipping as Jude. If we were to completely lose our footing and handgrip on the cables, we'd slide the distance to the nearest metal post below where we could right ourselves and regroup. The thought of this potential of slipping is intimidating enough, then amplified by the intense exposure that surrounds you once on the cables. We wouldn't have attempted it at all without being able to mitigate the serious risk of a fall by clipping into cables.

This Yosemite trip was special. I'm still in awe at our kids' good attitudes and major grit. I remember Jude's meditation in the van series (can't say it's relaxing, as I'm laughing hysterically every time, but love it), Violet finding and making art everywhere (nature's pom-poms), Story's witty one-liners, getting to see two of the cutest black bear cubs, and the kids helping me figure out crack climbing (they made it look easy while I was sure my ankles were breaking). Forever grateful for their bright, unique energy and this time I get with them, this time both Brandon and I get with them because together we've made this kind of time possible.

Shera commented on this Half Dome recap: "Incredible, Megs!!! Strong work you two, leading those girls and Jude! Such an amazing way to spend a day and to be a team and support one another and honor a teammate's decision. Gives me goosebumps."

Now, this coming from someone I deeply respect who practices all this better than anyone I know gave *me* goosebumps. We are forever a family, forever a team. We value and honor each other and the choices made by team members. I felt extra aware this adventure that such trips may be numbered. Aware Brandon or I may one day decide to pursue relationships that understandably complicate or change the dynamics of these kinds of trips. Maybe that will look like a partner of mine wanting clarification over sleeping arrangements on these adventures, or a partner of Brandon's joining us. I'm not even exaggerating— I'm open to expanded family vacations, expanded family Christmas mornings and birthday celebrations; I love this time with the kids too much to be inflexible and unwilling to share. I'm not sure what the future holds, but I am ready to cross those bridges as they come, ready to both make and respect new decisions, embrace new circumstances, and intentionally operate from an abundant and hopeful mindset while placing faith in our team family.

WITH GRACE AND GRATITUDE

Second-Guessing

It was over three months after this trip when Story called to me from her bedroom late one night. I had tucked her in at least half an hour earlier and was surprised she was still awake. I walked in, asked what's up, and she began to cry.

"I'm really sorry I didn't go all the way to the top of Half Dome," she sobbed. "We were so close and I made you miss it and I'm always the one asking to stop or turn around."

I'm not sure what triggered this. We'd been watching some rock climbing documentaries lately, maybe seeing Yosemite routes on the screen brought stuff up. She wasn't sure what made her think of it either, but I rarely see my rather easy-going, self-assured Story this rattled. I'm so glad 39-year-old, post-divorce me got to have this conversation.

"I can tell you're feeling really sad. You think you made it so I couldn't go to the top of Half Dome. You think you should have gone to the top since you were so close? Now wondering about that is making you sad?" Sitting on the edge of her bed and rubbing her back, I tried to mirror what she was telling me and validate her big feelings. "Can I tell you what I think, even if my perception is a little different from how you're feeling right now?" She agreed. "I think you are so, so brave. What you did was way braver than getting to the top. You are worried I was bummed to not get to the summit? Sweetie, I loved every minute with you. I could have hustled up after Dad, Jude, and Violet got back down and caught up to you guys later if I wanted; you didn't take that away, my goal for that adventure wasn't to get to the top but to spend a day hiking Yosemite together. I loved getting to watch you listen to *you*, you trust *you*, you choose and do what's best for *you*. It might get harder as you get older to not worry about what others think or about what outsiders say you should do, and that's normal. But I hope you never, ever feel that you need to apologize to me or anyone else for making a difficult decision that is right for you, that keeps you safe and happy."

Then I paraphrased one of my favorite reminders from Glennon Doyle: *Remember, it's your job to disappoint everyone else before disappointing yourself.* Story, being familiar with this advice (my kids have all heard me preach it often) and trusting it was wise, seemed a bit surprised I was implying that's what she'd done on Half Dome. She was calming some, tempted to entertain my response, but then quickly doubled down, listing all the reasons she should have just gone to the top, each one triggering more sobs than the last.

"It takes practice being kind to ourselves after making hard choices," I responded. "Our brains like second-guessing. It's normal to question if the other option would have been possible or better or made you happier. The problem with ignoring your core is sometimes the stakes are really high. It sounds like you're wondering if you should or could have chosen differently on those Half Dome cables. Yes, you likely would have been safe on that final climb to the top, but what matters more is how scary and unsafe it felt, and so you spoke up. I hope you keep doing that. Keep listening, keep asking questions, keep exploring what's right and best for you. I loved my day hiking Half Dome with you. You are nine years old and hiked over 18 miles up a big rocky mountain. I didn't see anyone else your age or height even looking at those cables from the sub-dome. You're a tiny-but-mighty total badass!"

She giggles, "Thanks, Mom, I love you."

"I love you bigger than the universe."

Three Things

> In the end, these things matter most: how much you loved, how gently you lived, and how gracefully you let go of things not meant for you. (Buddhist saying, most closely quoted in Kornfield 1994)

I used to think my divorce and the reasons behind it were life-defining failures. I was sure of it. At my lowest and darkest points, I couldn't see the point. I could remind myself to breathe, try to do the next right thing, be present with my kids—but rock bottom is pretty empty, and hope is hard to come by.

Loving big, living gently, letting go gracefully...I'm deeply grateful to have grown into this new perspective. I can now recognize my divorce as instrumental in learning and trying to honor these lovely things, gifting me a better understanding of what to do, pursue and prioritize in this precious window of being.

Take care of yourself, take care of each other, take care of kids who need unconditionally accepting, present, loving, authoritative parents no matter what hardship those parents are individually navigating. With grace and gratitude, continue showing up and trust the process.

ACKNOWLEDGMENTS

Who knew this acknowledgments page would be the most intimidating to write! I am overwhelmed and genuinely humbled at the outpouring of love and support I've received in the service of my goal to write this memoir.

Huge thanks to my incredible circle—dear friends and family, too numerous to name—but I see, love and appreciate you all immensely. From countless encouraging texts to keep writing, to sweet offers to purchase and review this book, to families of my Kindergarten students Venmoing their financial support to help get this book to the finish line; thank you, thank you!

Thank you Wandering Words Media, Carly Catt (Catt Editing) and Makenna Wallace for the editing, proofreading and citation support. Thank you Jessica Gleim for the generous marketing insight and direction. Thank you Shera Whitmer and Kelli Palma for volunteering not only editing services, but also honest feedback with regard to the personal content I was most apprehensive to share. That I could trust them to not only approach this project from a judgment-free space, but also to honor my goal of sharing this story with both integrity to myself and sensitivity to those I love was such a gift!

Lastly and largely, I feel immense gratitude to Brandon and our three kids. They've encouraged me to write and to share this story. They've never asked what exactly I was writing, never questioned if details I include are accurate and fair—they've just trusted me and understood this project mattered to me. I hope they always believe in and feel the huge love, trust, and respect I have for them in return—my tribe, my team, my heaven on earth. Thank you, I love you all so big!

REFERENCES

Allen, Emery. 2010. *Become*. North Carolina: lulu.com.

Anonymous. 2018. "Darling, You Deserve it All." @Nepenthe, October 3, 2018. https://www.facebook.com/Nepenthe.DZ/photos/a.992878550889643/1124988437678653/?type=3.

Bielanko, Serge. 2015. "You Can't Stay Married for the Kids." Yahoo Parenting. https://www.yahoo.com/news/you-cant-married-for-the-kids-119373232739.html?guccounter=1&guce_referrer=aHR0cHM6Ly93d3cuZ29vZ2xlLmNvbS8&guce_referrer_sig=AQAAAKl_VKkVnqKTawyZsdBmxZWK33plT0Su4ZqU htz6ia13WH2I2N8GW93B38RSMDUVAUIDzltA8bP5wHT M5nBMCR69PlTcHv4315SsBEnlN6OkBdglP2RtRtq0QgvoY-5irscXoe_l3f5pX3JVucWXqWfCJP_-ONA9B-zhSTu8ScVB.

Blommer, Katy. 2020. "The Working Mom Happiness Method." Women's Best Life University. https://www.womensbestlifeuniversity.com.

Blondin, Sarah. 2018. "Coming Home to Yourself." Insight Timer. https://insighttimer.com/meditation-courses/course_coming-home-to-yourself.

Broderick, Patricia, and Pamela Blewitt. 2020. "Middle Adulthood: Cognitive, Personality and Social Development." In *The Lifespan: Human Development for Helping Professionals*. 5th edition. Hoboken, NJ: Pearson Education, Inc.

Brown, Brené. 2010. *The Gifts of Imperfection: Let Go of Who You Think You Are Supposed to Be and Embrace Who You Are.* City Center, MN: Hazelden Publishing.

Brown, Brené. 2012. *Daring Greatly: How the Courage to be Vulnerable Transforms the Way We Live, Love, Parent and Lead.* New York: Barker and Taylor.

Brown, Brené. 2017. *Rising Strong.* New York: Spiegel and Grau.

Brown, Brené (@brenebrown). 2020. "Mark of a Wild Heart." Instagram, August 20, 2020. https://www.instagram.com/p/CEHpcHVD2XG/?utm_source=ig_web_copy_link&igsh=MzRlODBiNWFlZA==.

Brown, Brené. 2021. *Atlas of the Heart: Mapping Meaningful Connection and the Language of Human Experience.* New York: Random House.

Burrows, James, dir. 1996. *Friends.* Season 2, Episode 14, "The One with the Prom Video." Aired February 1, 1996 on NBC.

Campbell, Meghan. 2017. "Return to the Mountains." Trail Sisters. https://trailsisters.net/2017/05/16/return-to-the-mountains/.

Campbell, Meghan (@megbcampbell). 2018-2023. Private Instagram account entries.

Campbell, Meghan (@runwriteheal). 2018-2023. Private Instagram account entries.

Centers for Disease Control and Prevention. n.d. "Adverse Childhood Experiences (ACEs)." Accessed October 2, 2021: https://www.cdc.gov/vitalsigns/aces/index.html.

Dawkins, Richard. 2006. *The God Delusion.* Boston, MA: Mariner Books.

DiMicco, Kirk, and Chris Saunders, dir. 2013. *The Croods.* Beverly Hills, CA: Twentieth Century Fox Home Entertainment. DVD.

Doyle, Glennon. 2016. *Love Warrior: A Memoir.* New York: Flatiron Books.

Doyle, Glennon. 2020. *Untamed.* New York: The Dial Press.

Doyle, Glennon (@GlennonDoyle). 2021. "Brave is Matching Your Insides and Outsides." Instagram, August 21, 2021. https://www.instagram.com/p/CS2y2U2F8cs/?hl=en.

Doyle, Glennon. 2022. "How to come home to yourself with Martha Beck." *We Can Do Hard Things,* February 1, 2022. Podcast, audio, 58:00. https://podcasts.apple.com/us/podcast/how-to-come-home-to-yourself-with-martha-beck/id1564530722?i=1000549617997.

Emery, Robert. 2006. The *Truth About Children and Divorce: Dealing with the Emotions So You and Your Children Can Thrive.* New York: Plume.

Fridman, Lex. 2023. "Paul Conti: Narcissism, sociopathy, envy, and the nature of good and evil." *Lex Fridman Podcast,* February 7, 2023. Podcast, website, 3:17:28. https://www.youtube.com/watch?v=jRBksDVs4tg.

Fridman, Lex. 2023. "James Sexton: Divorce lawyer on marriage, relationships, sex, lies and love". *Lex Fridman Podcast,* September 17, 2023. Podcast, website, 3:44:36. https://www.youtube.com/watch?v=fUEjCXpOjPY.

Gilbert, Elizabeth. 2007. *Eat, Pray, Love: One Woman's Search for Everything Across Italy, India and Indonesia.* New York: Riverhead Books.

Gilbert, Elizabeth. 2016. *Big Magic: Creative Living Beyond Fear*. New York: Riverhead Books.

Gilbert, Elizabeth. n.d. "Come and Find me." Oprah.com. Accessed April 14, 2022: https://www.oprah.com/quote/elizabeth-gilbert-quote-come-and-find-me.

Gottman, John M. 1994. *Why Marriages Succeed or Fail: What You Can Learn from Breakthrough Research to Make Your Marriage Last*. New York: Simon & Schuster.

Hebb, Donald. 1949. *The Organisation of Behavior*. New York: John Wiley & Sons.

Hill, Jonah, dir. 2022. *Stutz*. Netflix. https://www.netflix.com/title/81387962.

Hollis, Rachel. 2020. *Didn't See That Coming: Putting Life Back Together When Your World Falls Apart*. New Work: Dey Street Books.

Humphreys, Alastair. 2012. "Microadventures." Alastair Humphreys: Living Adventurously. https://alastair-humphreys.com/microadventures-3/.

Kornfield, Jack. 1994. *Buddha's Little Instruction Book*. New York: Bantam Books.

LePera, Nicole. 2021. *How to Do the Work: Recognize Your Patterns, Heal from Your Past, and Create Yourself*. UK: Orion Spring.

LePera, Nicole (@the.holistic.psychologist). 2024. "Some of the Worst Advice." Instagram, February 9, 2024. https://www.instagram.com/p/C3JN3yxu3mW/?utm_source=ig_web_copy_link&igsh=MzRlODBiNWFlZA==.

Lusignan, Kerry. 2019. "Divorce is the Most Important Story You'll Ever Tell Your Child." The Gottman Institute. https://www.gottman.com/blog/divorce-is-the-most-important-story-youll-ever-tell-your-child/.

Malone, Adrian, dir. 1980-1981. *Cosmos: A Personal Voyage.* PBS.

Mandela, Nelson. n.d. "May Your Choices." Goodreads. Accessed August 21, 2022: https://www.goodreads.com/author/quotes/367338.Nelson_Mandela.

Mayol-García, Yeris, Benjamin Gurrentz, and Rose M. Kreider. 2021. "Number, Timing, and Duration of Marriages and Divorces: 2016." Current Population Reports, U.S. Census Bureau. https://www.census.gov/content/dam/Census/library/publications/2021/demo/p70-167.pdf.

McBride, Jean. 2016. *Talking to Your Kids about Divorce: A Parent's Guide to Healthy Communication at Each Stage of Divorce.* Texas: Althea Press.

Moore, Thomas quoted in Katherine Woodward Thomas. 2016. *Conscious Uncoupling: 5 Steps to Living Happily Even After.* New York: Harmony Books.

Moorjani, Anita. 2020. "Loving Yourself First." Facebook, December 27, 2020. https://www.facebook.com/Anita.Moorjani/photos/a.252465361465136/4078590992185868/?type=3.

Neff, Kristin. n.d. "What is Self-Compassion." Self-Compassion Dr. Kristin Neff. Accessed March 3, 2020: https://self-compassion.org/.

Nelson, Portia. 2012. *There's a Hole in My Sidewalk.* Anniversary Edition. Oregon: Atria Books/Beyond Word.

Okazaki, Chieko. 1998. *Disciples.* SLC, Utah: Deseret Book Company.

Oriah. 1999. *The Invitation.* San Francisco, CA: HarperONE.

Perez, Diego (@YungPueblo). 2023. "Relationship with Silence." X, September 11, 2023. https://twitter.com/YungPueblo/status/1701354013478850947.

Prochaska, James O., Sara Johnson, and Patricia Lee. 2009. "The Transtheoretical Model of behavior change." *The Handbook of Health Behavior Change.* New York: Spring Publishing Company.

Rand, Ayn. 1952. *Atlas Shrugged.* New York: Random House.

Rhoades, Galena K., Scott M. Stanley, and Howard J. Markman. 2010. "Should I Stay or Should I Go? Predicting Dating Relationship Stability From Four Aspects of Commitment." *Journal of Family Psychology* 24, no. 5: 543-550. https://doi.org/10.1037/a0021008.

Roosevelt, Theodore. 1910. "Citizenship in a Republic." Transcript of speech delivered in Paris, France, April 23, 1910. https://www.presidency.ucsb.edu/documents/address-the-sorbonne-paris-france-citizenship-republic.

Rosen, Michael. 1989. *We're Going on a Bear Hunt.* London, England: Walker Books.

Sagan, Carl. 1994. *Pale Blue Dot: A Vision of the Human Future in Space.* New York: Random House.

Shoffstall, Veronica A. 1971. *Comes the Dawn.* Newspaper clipping. (The following article by Patrick Wanis outlines the history and possible poem origins, accessed May 23, 2022: https://www.patrickwanis.com/you-learn-after-a-while-comes-the-dawn-the-poem-video-text-audio/.)

Shultz, Kathryn. 2011. *Being Wrong: Adventures in the Margin of Error*. New York: Ecco Press.

Siegel, Dan. 2021. "Wheel of Awareness." Dr. Dan Siegel: Inspire to Rewire. https://drdansiegel.com/wheel-of-awareness/.

Strayed, Cheryl. 2012. *Tiny Beautiful Things: Advice on Love and Life from Dear Sugar*. New York: Vintage Books.

Strayed, Cheryl. 2015. *Brave Enough*. New York: Alfred A. Knopf.

The Bowen Center for the Study of the Family. n.d. "Introduction to the Eight Components." Accessed April 10, 2022: https://www.thebowencenter.org/introduction-eight-concepts.

Thomas, Katherine W. 2016. *Conscious Uncoupling: 5 Steps to Living Happily Even After*. New York: Harmony Books.

Tippett, Krista. 2016. "Elizabeth Gilbert: Choosing curiosity over fear." *On Being*, July 7, 2016. Podcast, audio, 52:01. https://onbeing.org/programs/elizabeth-gilbert-choosing-curiosity-over-fear-may2018/.

Tippett, Krista. 2018. "Brene Brown: Strong back, soft front, wild heart." *On Being,* February 8, 2018. Podcast, audio, 51:32. https://onbeing.org/programs/brene-brown-strong-back-soft-front-wild-heart/.

Tolle, Eckhart. 1997. *Power of Now.* Vancouver, BC: Namaste Publishing.

Tolle, Eckhart. 2005. *New Earth*. New York: Dutton/Penguin Group.

Tolle, Eckhart (@eckharttolle). 2021. "Nothing Ever Happened in the Past." Instagram, March 9, 2021. https://www.instagram.com/p/CMM4Qu1lBAH/?hl=en.

Tyson, Neil deGrasse. 2017. *Astrophysics for People in a Hurry*. New York: W. W. Norton & Company.

Van der Kolk, Bessel A. 2014. *The Body Keeps the Score: Brain, Mind, and Body in the Healing of Trauma*. New York: Viking.

Waheed, Nayyirah. n.d. "All Hurt Someone." Quote Catalog. Accessed January 6, 2019: https://quote-catalog.com/communicator/nayyirah-waheed.

Made in the USA
Las Vegas, NV
30 January 2025

17233925R00129

VISIONS

DREAMS

AND HEALING

The Making of a Christian Counselor

R. Charles Bartlett

Acts 2:17 And it shall come to pass in the last days, saith God, I will pour out of My Spirit upon all flesh: and your sons and daughters shall prophesy, and your young men shall see visions, and your old men shall dream dreams.

xulon
PRESS